FOUNDATIONS OF
John Dewey's
Educational Theory

By MELVIN C. BAKER

KING'S CROWN PRESS 1955
COLUMBIA UNIVERSITY, NEW YORK

King's Crown Press

is an imprint established by Columbia
University Press for the purpose of making certain scholarly material available at
minimum cost. Toward that end, the pub-
lishers have used standardized formats
incorporating every reasonable economy
that does not interfere with legibility.
The author has assumed responsibility
for editorial style and for proofreading.

PUBLISHED IN GREAT BRITAIN, CANADA, INDIA, AND PAKISTAN
BY GEOFFREY CUMBERLEGE, OXFORD UNIVERSITY PRESS
LONDON, TORONTO, BOMBAY, AND KARACHI

MANUFACTURED IN THE UNITED STATES OF AMERICA

LIBRARY OF CONGRESS CATALOG CARD NUMBER: 55–7388

To Vaughn and Susan & the[ir]

Maternal grand parents,
Frank and Ossa Cha[...]
with the regards an[d]
respect of the author,

Melvin

July. 19

ACKNOWLEDGMENTS

As I CONTEMPLATE the events leading toward this publication, I find it difficult to limit citations other than to struggling humanity itself. Yet there are those, articulate with respect to this struggle, for whose direct aid I am deeply grateful. For whatever clarity of thought is expressed herein I am particularly indebted to the community of Professors K. D. Benne, of Boston University; B. O. Smith, W. O. Stanley, and A. W. Anderson, of the University of Illinois; and Bozidar Muntyan, of the University of Florida. From this community I received, also, unique individual contributions. In Professor Benne, with his extensive knowledge of both John Dewey's own works and those of his contemporaries, and his fertile insights into their possible implications, I had a guide in the realm of ideas such as few are so fortunate to have. Professor Smith gave me the courage to publish this material which I earnestly hope demonstrates some adequacies of response to his unforgettable lessons in straight thinking. My first clear insights into the significance of Dewey's ideas I owe to Professor Stanley, and to Professor Anderson I am similarly indebted for my first appreciation of the developmental period of Dewey's thought. In Professor Muntyan I have had a friend and intellectual companion responsible for much that may be most adequate, and for nothing inadequate, in this book.

I have received, too, another type of assistance in many ways no less valuable. For their encouragement and for their contributions to the practical conditions essential to the fulfillment of this enterprise I am especially indebted to Professors Hal G. Lewis and Vynce Hines, of the University of Florida,

to Dean J. R. Rackley, of the University of Oklahoma, and to Wilma, my wife.

In whatever ways I have been unable to realize the potentialities in all of these sources of aid, they are in no way responsible.

MELVIN C. BAKER

University of Florida
October, 1954

CONTENTS

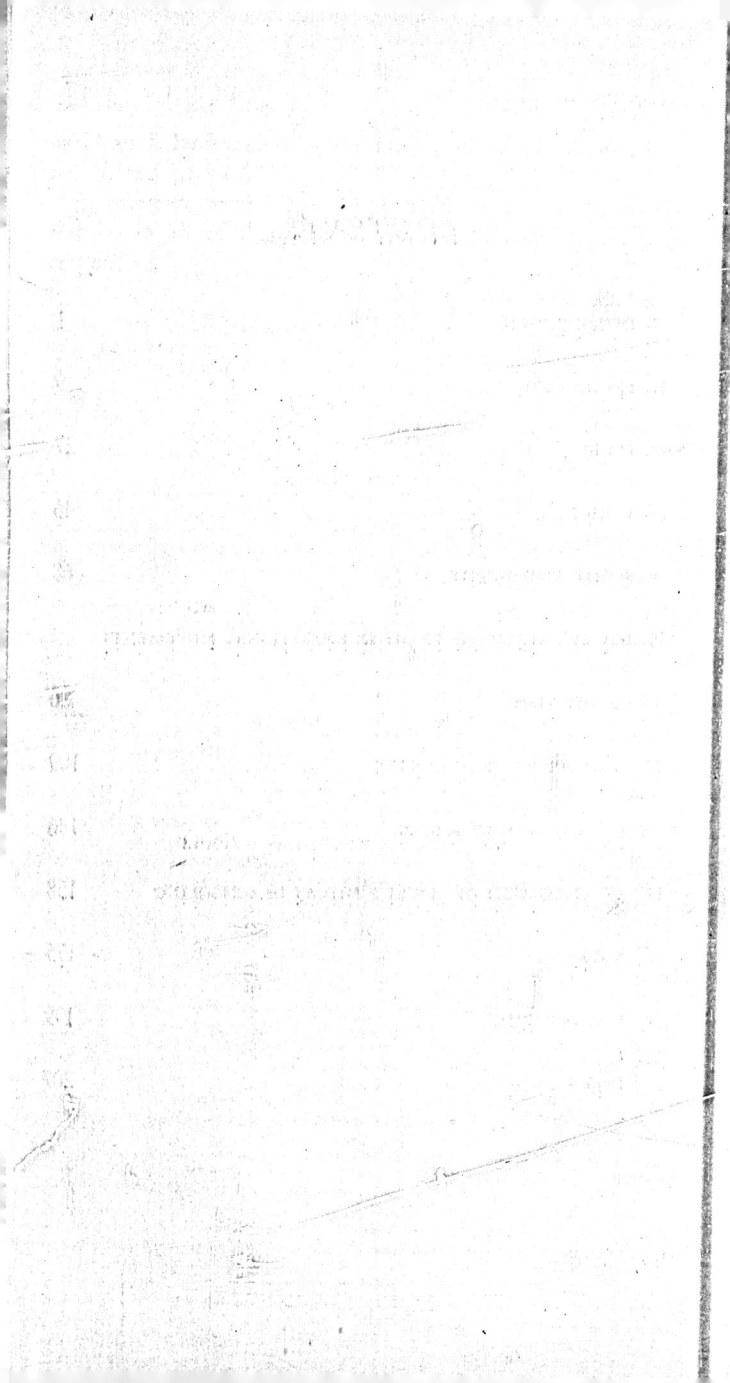

INTRODUCTION

IT IS AS WELL KNOWN as anything might be in the realm of
education that John Dewey's ideas have enjoyed wide influence
in educational thinking and discussion, both in America and
in other countries. Throughout the literature there are constant
references to his theories, and there is hardly an intelligent
discussion of the theory or practice of schooling which does
not, at some point and in some manner, take his suggestions
into account. Any genuine concern for the quality of our
educational processes and their products leads, then, to some
assessment of his theories. Help with this appraisal may right-
fully be expected from those writings which support and those
which attack his ideas, from those intended to interpret and
clarify his position, and from those which describe practices
purportedly derived from his theories. That such assistance is
available from these sources is, of course, undeniable. But it is
far from true that there is perfect agreement and understanding in all of the reflections and discussions involving Dewey's
ideas. On the contrary, it is evident that among his several
critics, as well as among his many followers, and between the
two groups, there are charges of misinterpretations which lead
to uncertainty and confusion in regard to the meanings he
sought to express.

As an illustration, Professor Ulich has seen a shift in Dewey's
thinking occurring about 1930. He implies that Dewey
wavered in his instrumentalism after this time and came more
to a faith in ideals lying beyond experimentation. Ulich has
written: "In the second period of his thought, Dewey's whole
conception of values received a character of definiteness which
lifts it out of mere experimentation into a sphere of persistent
validity."[1] On the other hand, Professor Childs writes that,

"for Dewey, the long search of man for a dependable method to control the course of his own intellectual activity has culminated in the logic of discovery and testing inherent in experimental inquiry."[2] From controversy at this level of thought to discussion of minute details of immediate procedures for schooling, there is obvious evidence of different interpretations of his theories by both friends and critics.

The same situation prevails in regard to the influence of Dewey's notions of schooling on actual school practices. It is commonly agreed that he has influenced the development of many new procedures. That he has, is quite probable; yet it is difficult to locate, with any certainty, the practices derived specifically from his theories. It has been popular to identify Dewey with what is new and different in twentieth-century education; but in the 1890's he wrote of the "new education" as opposed to traditionalism, and contrasted his own views with both. The "new education" he traced to the ideas of Rousseau, Pestalozzi, Froebel, and Herbart, and while he was in accord with some of their views, he also had his differences with them.[3] Among the waves of educational reform in recent decades it is hard to distinguish the new practices which follow from those aspects of the thought of these men with which Dewey agreed. It is equally difficult to discern the practices which accord with those aspects of their thought with which he differed. That these men also influenced such innovations as the "activity movement" and "progressive education" is clear; what is not certain is the extent to which Dewey's thought prevailed. The "project method" as another reform also can be traced to Dewey's ideas of schooling. But to what extent is this method more that of Kilpatrick, its popularizer, than Dewey's? To what extent has the "project method" been influenced by Morrison's notion of master of "units"? For it has been said that "even the more 'progressive' schools use 'units'; for the elaboration of the concept they are indebted to Professor Morrison."[4]

The difficulty involved in tracing modern practices in schooling to the influence of Dewey's theories is also seen in this
suggestion: "In a large measure, the early innovations were
protests against the evils of the traditional school." [5] In the
growing dissatisfaction with traditional education, the tendency, it has been pointed out, has been to seize upon anything new and different as something better than the old
with, perhaps, little attention to the underlying theories supporting the innovations. New ideas were accepted from any
quarter, just so they promised a move away from traditionalist
views. In a way, this may have represented the influence of
Dewey's experimentalist thought, but not necessarily experimentation guided by his theories. The point of confusion
comes, however, when innovators experiment indiscriminately
with respect to theory, yet claim that their practices are derivations from the ideas of Dewey. And the uncertainty is
heightened when conflict arises over interpretations of the
theoretical source they claim. According to Edwards and
Richey:

Although the progressives looked to Dewey as their leader, there
was great disagreement among them both with respect to philosophical principles and desirable school practice. Many of the pro-
fessed followers of Dewey read conflicting meanings out of his
writings. [6]

It seems necessary only to call attention to this lack of
common understanding of the meaning and relationship of
Dewey's ideas with respect to the various reforms of modern
schooling. If anything more need be said, one may refer to
Dewey's own charges that some of the practices claimed by his
followers as derived from his theories are based upon misinterpretations. Wahlquist, quoting from Dewey's *Experience
and Education,* says, "Professor Dewey then proceeds to casti-
gate progressive education as no one else has or could." [7] And
when Dewey's charges are read and the specific points of
misinterpretation are considered and weighed against even

slight familiarity with the derivations of school procedures in his own experimental school, the discrepancies are quite obvious. When we read that the Dewey School sought to organize as a miniature society, with the typical occupations of men both the method and content of schooling, we become aware of but a faint resemblance between what this brings to mind and the usual picture of "activities," "projects," and other "progressive" practices.

The situation is clearly thus: Dewey's philosophy, without question, has been so influential in twentieth-century thinking and discussion in regard to education as to be, if not always the focal point, of such force that any intelligent speculation or controversy has had to take it into account. Though exerting such influence, his ideas have been attacked by his critics and have been subjected to conflicting interpretations both by them and by his followers. It is probable that his ideas have also influenced innovations in school practices; just where, and to what extent, is difficult to determine. Practitioners of many new and different procedures in the schools make the claim that their operations are derived from Dewey's theories. Yet both his followers and Dewey himself have contended that some of the progressive trends are partial, inadequate, and perverse applications of his ideas. Finally, there are quite noticeable discrepancies between many of the procedures claimed as derivations of his ideas and the application of his theories as Dewey himself directed them in his experimental school.

Thus, among the barriers to a more adequate statement and resolution of the educational problems of our time is this perplexed situation. The chapters which follow record one approach toward meeting this difficulty. Their aim is to add some measure of clarification to the variously interpreted and widely misapplied ideas of John Dewey. They are focused upon the early development of his ideas as expressed in his writings during the period from about 1890 to 1904. Analyses of Dewey's thought, with the problem of education centrally

in mind, seem to have neglected this vantage point. Yet this is the period both of the formulation of Dewey's theoretical outlook and of his experiment with the school operations which he derived from his theories. From 1896 to 1904 he directed his experiment in what was then called the University of Chicago Laboratory School, now usually referred to as the Dewey School. Dewey has said that the school was a consequence of the philosophy which he, its director, held.

As that head was trained in philosophy and in psychology, the work of the school had a definite relation in its original conception to a certain body of philosophical and psychological conceptions. Since these conceptions had more to do, for better or worse, with the founding of the school than educational experience or precedent, an account of the actual work of the school would be misleading without a frank exposition of the underlying theory.[8]

This passage indicates that, in a sense, his school experiment was a culmination of the development of his theoretical point of view; it was founded upon his formulation of certain disciplines. It is well known that Dewey, the instrumentalist, originally held to absolute idealism. It is in this period, 1890–1904, that this shift occurred in his thinking; it is the period of his struggle to reach and crystallize his experimental point of view.

A recent study made by Morton G. White has shown how fruitful for an understanding of Dewey's logical theory an inquiry into this formative period can be.[9] White ably located the origin of Dewey's instrumental logic and traced the shift in his thinking as he reached this position from an original Hegelian standpoint. The successful added clarification which White has contributed to an understanding of Dewey's logical theory through the method of tracing the intellectual aspects of his development supports the soundness of a suggestion made by Herbert Schneider. The latter, commenting on the fact that students laid aside the works of Locke for those of Kant, and Kant's for those of Hegel, said:

I mean to call attention not so much to the mere fact that philosophic schools change, and with them their textbooks, as to the more significant fact that the next generation never knows *why* the change was made. The next generation did not see Kant against a background of Locke, nor McCosh against Comte and Spencer. In the same way students today are reading the books which Professor Dewey has written and not the books he has read.[10]

The significance of this statement, together with White's demonstration of its fruitfulness, lends support to the notion that a clearer understanding of Dewey's educational theory can be achieved through a study of this formative period in his intellectual development focused upon that theory and the school practices derived from it. Schneider's order, perhaps, calls for too much; but if students cannot read all of the books that Dewey read, they can, it seems, still profit by reading them through his eyes, as expressed in his reactions and criticisms.

This relative neglect of the formative period in the development of his ideas on education extends to a similar lack of careful consideration of the experimental school in which Dewey attempted to translate into practice the ideas he was developing during this period. True, there have been many fleeting references to his school, and some more extensive elaborations of its theory and practices.[11] But these only seem to raise more questions than they clarify. And in the literature reflecting the thinking and discussion involving the controversies over the meaning of Dewey's ideas and their implications for practice, there is brought to bear little evidence from the Laboratory School. It is important, in view of this neglect, to examine this evidence, and promising, it is believed, to focus upon it as the culmination of the formative period in Dewey's intellectual development.

In line with Dewey's statement that the school was based upon philosophical and psychological conceptions he held at

the time, we begin with an examination of his formulation of the foundational disciplines. Chapters II, III, IV, and V record the development of his thought in Psychology, Logic, Ethics, and Social Philosophy. In dealing with each, other theories, then current, are contrasted with Dewey's early idealistic position and the reconstruction of his own theories is shown in his shift toward instrumentalism. During the same period of this development Dewey was active in various educational movements. In chapter VI his reactions and criticisms with respect to these movements are examined. Discernible in these writings is the reciprocal developmental influence of his "philosophical and psychological conceptions" and his educational speculations on each other. In chapter VII the fruition of his inquiries is shown in his formulation of the problem of education and in his hypothesizing for the solution of this problem. There emerges a view of the functions of his "philosophical and psychological conceptions" in pointing to the problem, as supports for the possibility for its solution, and as guides for the theory of schooling. Together, these illustrate what Dewey saw as the requirements for educational theory. In chapter VIII some of the practices Dewey himself derived from his theory of schooling are observed, with particular attention to the role of the theory as a guide for the procedures developed in the Dewey School. In the final chapter, Dewey's theory and practice of schooling, as formulated and applied at the time of his Laboratory School, are assessed through four modes of evaluation. One consideration is the consistency of his theory of schooling with his formulation of the foundational disciplines. The significance of a theory of schooling with relation to the social situation it is designed to meet requires an examination of the adequacy and completeness of the diagnosis of that situation. The school itself in its operations is assessed for the congruence of the application with the theory from which it is derived. And finally, since by Dewey's own position a theory must be tested by acting upon it, the school is considered for its function as a test of the theory of schooling.

It is probably impossible to clarify all the impressions of meaning which come from an inquiry such as this. Particularly does this seem so in the case of one with Dewey's stature and his breadth and depth of meaning. He is such a fertile source for insight; he offers such a wealth of suggestion. Turning now to his psychology, both this fact and the restriction to the formative period in the development of his thought are to be kept in mind. So, too, is an ultimate concern with our current educational procedures and outcomes.

PSYCHOLOGY

THE DEVELOPMENT of John Dewey's thought emerged from a background of academic experiences in his undergraduate work at the University of Vermont and graduate study at the, then, new Johns Hopkins University. In the latter institution, among his teachers were the Hegelian, Morris; Hall, a disciple of Wundt and experimental psychology; and Peirce, at the time concerned apparently with formal logic. The Administration of the school emphasized science, perhaps at the expense of philosophy. The situation has been described thus: "We have before us a picture of Dewey coming to Johns Hopkins in 1882, studying under teachers who expounded absolute idealism, experimental psychology, formal logic, and the philosophy of science." [1]

Now this is a rather varied mixture, indicative in a way of the end of one era and the beginning of a new. In psychology this transition can be denoted as the passage from philosophical to experimental psychology, if we use Brubacher's terms. "During the last quarter of this century psychology passed from a philosophical to a scientific discipline." [2] Of the former type, the so-called philosophical, there were two principal varieties still retaining considerable vigor. One of these was the sensationalism of British Empiricism; the other was the idealistic psychology of Hegelianism.

Dewey originally supported idealism, in opposition to the empiricist's passive wax-tablet theory of mind; at the same time he remained quiet but alert in regard to experimental psychology. In one of his first books, in a commendation of the views of Leibniz, he expressed his early attachments: "Such thoughts as that substance is activity; that its process is measured by its end, its idea; that the universe is an interrelated unit; the thoughts of organism, of continuity, of uniformity of law—introduced and treated as Leibniz treated them, are imperishable." [3]

In this appreciation of activity, continuity, and organism rested Dewey's opposition to sensationalistic psychology. The latter stemmed from Locke's banishment of innate ideas from the mind, henceforth to be conceived as a blank sheet of paper. While the meaning of Locke's theory is still open to examination, common interpretation had it that this mind was passive, awaiting the impress from some outside object through the medium of the senses. There was no continuity in the receipt of these impressions; each was a distinct, atomistic sensation, and mental life became, as with Hume, nothing but a succession of mental states. For one such as Dewey, who leaned toward the Leibnizian view that "substance is activity, that its process is measured by its end, its idea," a psychology of mere association of mental states could in no way explain or measure activity. If the end of individual feeling or desire is a mental state, and if the end of ideation is but some reshuffling of these states, there is no clear explanation for activity; furthermore, there is no measure by which either the individual or others may judge the activity.

Dewey's difficulty with sensationalistic psychology, then, is its failure to give an adequate explanation of the relations of thought, feeling, and action either within or between individuals. For the problem he saw was how the individual consciousness shares with others common knowledge, purposes, and values. In his first approach to the problem he takes the Hegelian viewpoint and defines psychology as the science "of the reproduction of some universal content or existence, whether of knowledge or of action, in the form of individual, unsharable consciousness." [4] There is, as he saw it then, a universal consciousness which the individual actively seeks to decipher or realize. "The individual consciousness is but the process of realization of universal consciousness through itself.

Looked at as a process, as realizing, it is individual consciousness; looked at as produced or realized, as conscious of the
process, that is, of itself, it is universal consciousness." [5]

We shall see later, in Dewey's criticisms of the psychology of
W. T. Harris, the specific objections he comes to hold against
this view he first accepted to combat sensationalistic psychology. Here we shall turn to the development of his thinking
which finally led to those objections. For Dewey had rejected
the Hegelian view by the time he began his school experiment. This does not mean that he discards the emphasis upon
activity, continuity, and organism; rather, it means that he
succeeds in reconstructing these conceptions. That they are
the origin of many of his later ideas is ably shown by White,
who accounts for Dewey's changing perspective by a twist the
latter made in a method he approved in Leibniz. Commenting
on the view of organism and life radical to the thought of
Leibniz, Dewey had said, "I do not think, however, that it
can truly be said that he was led to the idea simply from the
state of psychological investigation at that time. Rather, he
had already learned to think of the world as organic through
and through, and found in the results of biology confirma-
tions, apt illustrations of a truth of which he was already
convinced." [6] White's analysis shows that while Dewey at
first also saw the results of empirical science only as apt illustrations of his theories, he later changed his method of using
these results. "What is distinctive in Dewey's development is
that because of careful attention to results in biology, sociology,
and psychology, he saw that they were only superficial con-
firmations of idealism and that a recognition of their true
significance would lead to the abandonment of idealist organ-
icism." [7]

This newer method is not apparent in the *Psychology* of
1887 or in the *Applied Psychology* written with J. A. McLellan
in 1889. It is not until we study his articles appearing in the
1890's that we begin to see the principle at work and discover

the psychological theory which served as one of the foundations of his experimental school. A short book review written in 1891 seems to imply the direction of his thinking at the opening of the decade. With more disdain than was customary for him, he criticized *Elementary Psychology* by J. H. Baker after the fashion of the idealists in reviewing a work suffering from empirical influence. He found nothing good in it except that it was an apt description of the psychology underlying current pedagogy. He said, "Upon the whole, the book is, in form and substance, an admirable reflection of the ideas and methods of the vast bulk of our teachers who are earnestly striving, along the lines of the ordinary pedagogy of our normal schools and teachers' institutes, to elevate education. To discuss, therefore, its substance would be to go beyond the limits of a review of this book into the question of the value, scientific and educational, of the current psychology." [8] He implied that he knew what teachers were thinking and doing, that it was inadequate, and that perhaps the time had come to reexamine psychology not only as a science but also for its implications for education. He was ready to take upon himself this task of reconstruction equipped with what had become a distinctive feature of his inquiry: he looked to the methods and products of other sciences and scholars.

Two primary sources from which he drew were, first, biology through Darwinian evolution, particularly as the latter was being used in sociology, and second, physiology as it supported the psychology of William James. The former led Dewey to a notion of psychology as a social science, through a reinterpretation of Darwin's theory of conflict. White gives us the significance of Darwin's influence on Dewey in this comment:

He begins with the Hegelian concept of conflict as we have noted. Philosophy, according to his 1884 paper on Kant, began with "contradictions." From them, by Hegelian synthesis, the solutions emerge. He then rides very easily on the wave of a newly gained

naturalism into the Darwinian conflict doctrine. Man achieves intelligence in the course of a struggle for existence; again conflict. But now we come to the specifically Deweyan notion of conflict— the conflict, or tension, which characterizes human behavior in a problematic situation. The march is intricate and exciting— from Hegel to Darwin to Dewey.[9]

From this we get the suggestion of the shift from the idea of individuals coming to participate in an existing universal consciousness to the notion of individuals creating a common intelligence through problem-solving activities.

The second influence is suggested in this comment by William James:

I have tried to show that all Reasoning depends on the ability of the mind to break up the totality of the phenomenon reasoned about into partial factors or elements, and to pick out from among these the particular one which, in our given theoretical or practical emergency, may lead to the proper conclusion.[10]

Here is the notion of the mind as an instrument for guidance in on-going experiences and not for realizing an existing consciousness. Dewey also received help from James in developing a non-idealistic opposition to sensationalistic psychology. James wrote:

These mental functions are already at work in the first beginning of sensation and the simplest changes of sensation moreover involve consciousness of all the categories—time, space, number, objectivity, causality. There is not first a passive act of sensation proper—followed by an active production or projection ("inference") of the attributes of objectivity by the mind. These all come to us together with the sensible qualities, and their progress from vagueness to distinctness is the only process psychologists have to explain.[11]

With such suggestions from the ideas of Darwin, James, and others, Dewey set about the development of his own positive psychology, which was rather completely formulated by the time of his experimental school. We shall see the

notions of conflict and instrumentalism as they are used by
Dewey in the statement of his newer position.

CONFLICT AND INSTRUMENTALISM IN SOCIAL PSYCHOLOGY

In a review of four books under the title "Social Psychology," we find Dewey's newer psychological insights appearing
in his comments on Lester Ward's *The Psychic Factors of
Civilization* and Benjamin Kidd's *Social Evolution*.[12] Ward's
book was an attempt to state the foundations of a sociology
definitely based upon psychological methods and data. As
Dewey describes it, Ward's thesis is that the force which keeps
society moving is the feelings taken collectively, and the
power which gives direction is the intellect. But this conception of the forces in society rests upon a false psychology of
feeling and action. Because, Dewey declares, Ward sets up a
dualism where sensation and idea are two distinct things, he
not only gets himself involved in contradiction but must get
action out of passive states of feeling. He says, "Let the fundamental thing be conceived as impression resulting from contact
with an object, and thought, perception, must be another
sort of thing; desire and action can be brought in from passive
feeling only by a virtual contradiction, while nature, the individual, and society have independent ends." [13] Dewey does not
like this separation of ends and explains that Ward got to
this position by the insertion of a passive impression between
the "object" and the feeling and idea. The corrective psychology needed is given:

Let once the standpoint of *action* be taken and there is a continuous process; the sensory ending is a place, not for receiving sensations and starting notions on their road to the mind, but a place
(viewed from the standpoint of nature) for transforming the
character of motion; the brain represents simply a further development and modification of action and the final motor discharge
(the act proper) the completion of this transformation of action.[14]

A little later he says:

Mr. Ward is so under the spell of an old psychology of sensation that he fails to recognize the radical psychological fact, although just the fact needed to give firm support to his main contentions— I mean *impulse,* the primary fact, back of which, psychically we cannot go.[15]

Here, then, is the base or matrix from which Dewey develops his psychology; the impulse is primary and its development through a continuous process into a complete act is the proper focus for psychologists. Instead of sensations, feelings, ideas, and actions as separate forces with different ends, we have unified force in impulse, with unified ends in felt functional activity.

But this is not all we get from Dewey's review of Mr. Ward. The latter has a theory of the evolution or growth of intelligence which Dewey approves. It begins with the evolutionary theory of conflict aroused as the organism strives to satisfy desire. Since all desires cannot be satisfied directly, a variety of attacks are attempted out of which the one most advantageous is selected. This selection is not blind but leads to the power of mental exploration. When the conflict is with other organisms, the reaction is apt to be egoistic and direct. But the development of mental exploration occurs when the conflict is with inanimate objects and intelligence becomes objective, impersonal, and disinterested. So it is through the mediation of invention that intelligence works free from subjection to the demands of personal desire.

It sets up its own interest, its own desire, which is comprehension of relations as they are. Scientific discovery and speculative genius are simply farther steps on this same road.[16]

At this point Ward seems to find conflict eliminated. And here Dewey finds Mr. Kidd's book a necessary corrective, for Kidd declares progress is always effected through competition and struggle. With Kidd we have blind conflict; with Ward we have intelligence freed from the conditions which originated it. Dewey abstracts conflict from the one and intelligence from the other. He says:

> To me it appears as sure a psychological as biological principle that men go on thinking only because of practical friction or strain somewhere, that thinking is essentially solution of tension. . . . The elimination of conflict is, I believe, a hopeless and self-contradictory ideal. Not so the directing of the struggle to reduce waste and to secure its maximum contribution. It is not the sheer amount of conflict, but the conditions under which it occurs that determine its value. Mr. Kidd seems practically to ignore this possibility of increasing control of conflict and to leave the individual at its mercy; the individual according to him, is a tool of the conflict in evolving progress, not the conflict a tool of man.[17]

If we summarize the psychological principles Dewey sets forth in this review, we have first an organism with an impulse for action; action is in no sense reaction to a passively received extrinsic impression or idea—at most these are but divisions of labor in a complete act; action on the part of an organism leads to conflict with other active organisms and the world of inanimate objects; this conflict prohibits direct satisfaction of the ends of impulse; therefore, the need for indirect response develops into intelligent recognition of ends and their means of attainment; this intelligent direction is simplified in conflict with the nonsentient world and, through the mediation of invention, it becomes objective and impersonal; while indirection is more difficult to achieve in social conflict, this same objectivity can be developed so that legislation of social forces is the same as the principle of invention in dealing with physical factors.

CONFLICT AND INSTRUMENTALISM IN THE CIRCUIT OF THE ACT

The concept of conflict Dewey accepts here may appear to have such prominence only in his social psychology. But we

find this principle also in a discussion of strictly individual psychology in a paper published in 1896, called "The Reflex Arc Concept." [18] As we may expect, Dewey is again criticizing the separation of stimulus and response into independent entities. Again he insists that they are divisions of labor, parts of what he now calls a complete coordination. Conflict arises within the coordination.

The circle is a co-ordination, some of whose members have come into conflict with each other. It is the temporary disintegration and need of reconstitution which occasions, which affords the genesis of, the conscious distinction into sensory stimulus on one side and motor response on the other. The stimulus is that phase of the forming co-ordination which represents the conditions which have to be met in bringing it to a successful issue; the response is that phase of one and the same forming co-ordination which gives the key to meeting these conditions, which serves as instrument in effecting the successful co-ordination. They are therefore strictly correlative and contemporaneous. The stimulus is something to be discovered, to be made out; if the activity affords its own adequate stimulation, there is no stimulus save in the objective sense already referred to. As soon as it is adequately determined, then and then only is the response also complete. To attain either means that the co-ordination has completed itself. Moreover, it is the motor response which assists in discovering and constituting the stimulus.[19]

If we retrace our steps from the primary fact of impulse, we find in the original act what may be distinguished as stimulus. Rather, we should say that the action discovers or constitutes the stimulus. But simultaneously, to discover the stimulus is to constitute the response. Within the coordination there develops a new set of conditions to be constituted into a second stimulus and response and so on in continuous activity. But each act is problematical in that there is conflict over the constitution of its stimulus and response phases. Any on-going series of activities may provide its own adequate stimulation out of these conflicts. Thus it is in the very conditions of life itself

that man is at least a problem forming animal, in conflict with
himself over the constitution of the problems and with himself
and the rest of nature in their solution.

Emotion

It may seem from this description that all conflict is resolved
into problems by the mere intellect and solved by the intellect.
If so, is there no place for the psychological concepts of emotion, attitude, instinct, interest, and habit? Dewey fits these
into his theory of coordination in two articles in which he
claims to reconstruct the James-Lange theory of emotions with
the aid of Darwin's theory of evolution. These appear under
the titles "The Theory of Emotion. I. Emotional Attitudes," [20]
and "The Theory of Emotion. II. The Significance of Emotions." [21]

Here again we find that "the mode of behavior is the
primary thing and that the idea and the emotional excitation
are constituted at one and the same time; that, indeed, they
represent the tension of stimulus and response within the
co-ordination which makes up the mode of behavior." [22] Thus
there are no atomic elements such that we receive an impression of a bear, followed by emotional excitation of the bear as
frightful, followed by the idea of running from the bear, and
then the actual running. Nor does the emotional excitation
come after the running. These are mere functional distinctions made in our interpretations. Instead, "The hypothesis
here propounded is that the factors of a co-ordination . . .
begin to operate and we run away; running away we get the
idea of 'running-away-from-bear,' or of 'bear-as-thing-to-be-run-
from.'" [23] Note that not only idea and emotion but action are
involved. If we were completely immobilized there would be
no coordination; therefore, there would be no emotion, only
a pathological state of shock. So emotion is not a thing apart;
it is an intrinsic part of all activity and is always about or

toward something; it always has its "object" or intellectual content.

Now there are acts that are repeated over and over as activities complete in themselves. These gradually become reduced or absorbed in larger activities until the original act becomes an attitude of instinctive reaction. As attitude it is that which was a complete act but is no more. As instinct it is an impulse to react to its associated stimulus—a tendency thoroughly ingrained in the system. When this instinctive attitude tends to be assertive in a more comprehensive act it conflicts with present necessities made known in perception or idea. Emotion here becomes the adjustment or tension of the habit or instinctive reaction with the ideal.

Interest and Effort; Desire and Motive

As may be expected, interest is not something apart from activity but is the feeling which arises with the completed coordination.

Interest is undisturbed action, absorbing action, unified action and all interests, as interests, are equally interesting . . . that principle which secures that if only full or organic activity go into each end, each act shall equally satisfy in its time and place, is the highest ethical principle.[24]

This theory of interest is more fully developed in "Interest in Relation to Training of the Will." [25] Dewey shows that the current doctrines, of interest on one hand, and of effort on the other, stem from the identical assumption that the idea or object to be mastered, the end to be reached, the act to be performed, is external to the self.[26] He opposes this separation because,

The genuine principle of interest is the principle of the recognized identity of the fact or the proposed line of action with the self, that it lies in the direction of the agent's own growth and is therefore, imperiously demanded, if the agent is to be himself.[27]

Interest is already in or with the organism; it is dynamic. It attaches itself to objects with the accompaniment of a feeling of their worth or an internal realization of their value. Interest is both immediate, where energy is put forth for its own sake, or mediate, where the end becomes somewhat remote. In the latter case effort and desire exist. These, like emotion, previously discussed, are involved in the state of tension that exists between the ideal in view and the present actual state of things. Thus we arrive at these definitions:

The tendency of the end to realize itself through the process of mediation, overcoming resistance, is effort. The tendency of the present powers to continue a struggle for complete expression in an end remote in time is desire.[28]

And when the means of attainment become identified with the end, desire is translated into motive, a motive for effort in realizing the end.[29] In life there are plenty of obstacles and difficulties to be overcome, conflicts and problems to be solved. Interests must be worked out and in doing so "will" is developed. There is no place for a "will that wills will," as W. T. Harris expressed it.[30]

Imagination

There is at least one further very important relationship in Dewey's organic conception of the coordination, that between imagination and expression. We have already seen that though ideal and act may be distinguishable, in actuality they are simultaneous reenforcements of each other. In no sense do we get an ideal and then proceed to its expression, for the ideal cannot be conceived in terms other than the way it is to be expressed. There is both a short- and long-term phase to the idea of coordination; or better, there are short-term coordinations within an on-going comprehensive activity. A primitive coordination is of the former variety, and is typical of early childhood when activity is its own end. It is when the

child develops the power to distinguish ends and means that he has more extensive coordinations. This developing "power" is really the imagination. Now in the earlier period, image or ideal and overt act are one. But in the later stage, within the comprehensive coordination as distinct from its final consummation, two kinds of images are one. That is, we have an image of the ideal together with an image of the expression of the ideal. It is doing but not necessarily overt doing; it is doing in imagination and reflection, although to repeat for emphasis, the final consummation would involve overt action. Dewey says:

We cannot speak of an idea *and* its expression; the expression is more than a mode of conveying an already formed idea; it is part and parcel of its formation.[31]

And again he says:

The mental occurrence which represents the form or mode of expression is just as much an image as is the idea itself. It is not the problem of the relation of a spiritual image to a physical organ of expression but of one sort of imagery to another.[32]

This means that just as act and ideal or technique and content are interacting elements, each reconstructing the other, so too are these two kinds of images reconstructing each other in imagination. This permits the extension of experience beyond the bounds of present sensibilities; it is growing intelligence.[33]

SOME IMPLICATIONS FOR EDUCATION

One way to help clarify the meaning and significance of an idea is to consider the possible consequences of its use as a guide to action. Hence, it seems advantageous to attempt this mode of clarification here, and also after the discussion of the other foundational disciplines in the next three chapters. At least two hazards accompany this venture. One is that different shades of meaning, tentatively held, may suggest different operations. The other is that a single idea, or set of ideas, may be part of a larger system of ideas; consequently, different procedures may be implied when the idea is seen in wider context. The latter is particularly true with Dewey's ideas; for, as emphasized later, his psychological ideas are interrelated with those of the other disciplines.

Awareness of these precautions is one safeguard in drawing and weighing possible implications. But there are also guides available. In the case of Dewey's psychological thought, his own practical derivations in his experimental school are available in forecast. Then, too, his criticisms of the alternate sets of psychological ideas include what he saw as their implications for practice. Finally, logic, to the degree that it is sound, warrants some conclusions. With these precautions and guides in mind, perhaps clearer meaning of Dewey's struggle to reformulate psychological views can be achieved by contrasting some of their implications for education with some of those suggested by sensationalistic and idealistic psychologies.

The sensationalistic psychology which Dewey opposed separates, as we have seen, thought from feeling; it hardly explains the relations of either to action; it neglects a social psychology. Education based upon this psychology, then, apparently starts from without the individual. He must be provided a stimulus, presented an object, in order for the process of learning or behavior to begin. The stimuli to be presented would be selected by a teacher, and probably those of greatest worth and desirability are selected by the teacher, or some other source outside the child. There seems to be no significant principle to guide the selection of the subject-matter to be presented. Some material may tend predominantly to produce a variety of sensations; some may contribute to a greater or more elaborate arrangement of ideas resulting from impression; and some, presumably, will bring about immediate activity. Therefore, the principle followed might require equal amount of subject-matter directed to each of these phases; or

it might demand greater attention to subject-matter which will stimulate that one phase considered by the teacher as most important. This presentation can, of course, be made to groups of individuals, but the impressions received, the ideas arising, and their manipulation are strictly an individual matter.

The idealistic psychology which Dewey first approved contrasts with this passive, atomistic, and mechanistic approach; it postulates an active, continuous, and organic development, thought of as self-realization. In the latter view the individual was seen as active, as motivated by feeling and desire, and as striving to reproduce the universal consciousness. To reach this state of near union of the self with the wisdom and spiritual ideals of the absolute is a long, tedious journey. The same feelings that motivate the individual also may lead him astray unless, presumably, they are carefully disciplined by others until such time as his own intellect and will arise to control his desires. And before the individual is able to understand the institutions of men which embody the ideals of the absolute, he must acquire the tools of learning and the information with which intellect and will, when finally developed in early adulthood, can contrive to form into spiritual wisdom. Education, then, seems to be such that the teachers discipline the emotional life of the child, train him in the tools of learning, see that he appropriates a wide range of items of information, and finally, with the necessary equipment and the newly arisen intellect and will at hand, permit him to continue the process of realizing himself under his own power and control. Thus the teacher's role in assisting the process of self-realization appears to be marked out in stages; first, discipline the child in moral ideas and virtues; second, train him in the formal tools of learning; third, teach him the products of knowledge; and fourth, encourage him in the development of wisdom.

Set off from the educational implications following from

these psychologic views, we find three requirements for education set by Dewey's reconstruction of psychology. In the first place, since the individual is an active creature moved by impulse, the educative process begins from within; it is self-initiated. And since there is no separation of the phases of experience, the impulse is ideally sustained by feeling, guided by thought, and expressed in action. This is ideally so, because the individual is in interaction with his environment and conditions may be such as to break this continuity. Education, then, must be assisted by teachers who set the conditions for this continuity and guide it in process. Thus children are to be allowed to institute the expression of their impulses and then are guided through the process of a complete act of experiencing. There can be no separate training for one phase of experience at a time, or no delayed attention to one phase until others are developed; the total process is possible and should be provided for from the beginning, the difference in earlier and later periods being only one of the degree of complexity of surroundings within which experiencing occurs. Therefore education begins with the child engaging in familiar activities, expressing his impulses in acquired modes of response. From the notion of conflict, it is clear that the child encounters obstacles and barriers to his on-going expression; he is forced to make choices, decisions; he may do this spontaneously at first, only to meet greater difficulties; so thought arises to guide his mediation of these conflicts and his actions become deliberate. Thus the child learns in situations where his interests are involved and he must surmount difficulties by forming and solving the problems that must be met if he is to fulfill his purposes. Therefore, the teacher must guide the child in problem-solving situations. Furthermore, since the experience gained in any situation must be relative to past and future experiences if the desired continuity is to be attained, the situations, themselves, must have this quality of relationship. Occupations provide both the problem element and con-

tinuing integral relationships and so are selected as the method of guiding the learning process in accord with the psychological nature of the child.

The second requirement for education follows from this first one; if the method of guiding the child in the educative process centers in the child's active engagement in occupations, then occupations are also the content of education. For, as we have seen, impulse is no abstract, separate event; it is particular, concrete, and always directed toward some object or content. So if impulses are expressed in occupations, they are also expressed toward occupations. We have seen that the child institutes the learning process from within by acting toward his familiar environment in modes of response to which he has become accustomed. It is, then, in and toward the occupations of his home life that he expresses his interests; here is the early content of his learning. The home occupations are related to wider occupations in social life, and to all the institutions of cultural life. In the same way the content of education expands from its starting point in home occupations. Since the active learner engages in occupations, it is in processes that he is concerned, with products being the end point or goal. Thus, the content grows through the processes of occupations and the development of all the institutional devices and procedures arising from and related to these, and on to the resultant products of knowledge and ideals. The subject-matter of education, then, consists of the products of adult knowledge and wisdom, not as ready-made presentations or objects of appropriation, but as guides for the teacher as the child is led to understand their meaning in relation to the processes by which they were developed.

The third requirement is set by the element of conflict in social psychology. The expression of impulse occurs in situations which are predominantly social. Conflict arises as one being limits or forces restrictions of the expressions of another. We have seen that it is this fact that causes the individual to think and to continue thinking, and thus is essential to learning. Therefore, education is a social matter and must proceed in a social setting. The nature of this setting is crucial, for while conflict is the source of thought, the conditions under which it occurs must be such that it leads to the mediation of impulses of all concerned so that the expressions of each realize his self-interests. Otherwise, if for no other reasons, the psychological nature of the child will be violated.

But there are other reasons, as is implicit in all of Dewey's struggle with a reinterpretation of psychology. We have only to recall his early praise of Leibniz's views of organism and his postulation of a universal consciousness which individual consciousness strove to reproduce to see that Dewey's newer psychology had to support an adequate explanation of the relation of the individual to the group and therefore must be integrated with a social philosophy. We have seen that the full or complete psychological act is also the ethical act; obviously the psychology of interaction and continuity must fortify a concept of ethics that guides the development of this relationship. And finally, Dewey's dissatisfaction with both sensationalistic and idealistic explanations for the origin and function of thought indicates that a more adequate account is required and one with which logical explanations of feeling and action must be consistent. So, while much more might be said concerning the possible implications for education which stem from Dewey's psychology, since the latter is but a portion of the conceptual structure from which Dewey's educational theory is derived, further analysis will await an examination of his theories of social philosophy, ethics, and logic.

LOGIC

AN APPRAISAL of Dewey's position on logic at the time of his experimental school must consider the fact that his *Studies in Logical Theory* did not appear until 1903, the last year of his school. After opening the decade of the nineties with a series of four articles appearing in 1890 and 1891,[1] he published nothing more specifically on the subject of logic until 1900, when he wrote "Some Stages of Logical Thought."[2] But it seems fair to include the ideas expressed in both of the later works in a statement of Dewey's position at the time of his school. For in the 1890's, as White insists, "his silence on logical matters was no proof that he was not working on problems which he considered logical. He had been teaching courses in logic, in connection with which he had been studying the texts of Mill, Lotze, Bosanquet, and Bradley."[3] White also, in discussing Dewey's shifting outlook, reminds us of a letter written by Dewey to William James in 1903. Dewey was replying to a question James had asked concerning the origin of the "new school of thought" at Chicago. He said: "As for the standpoint we have all been at work at it for about twelve years."[4] It seems safe to assume that Dewey's thinking on logic in 1896 reflected the same kind of reconstruction of his earlier idealistic thought as did his psychology.

To get at a proper perspective for Dewey's "newer thought" on logic, we must see briefly what other theories there were. He originally held to the idealists' views on the state of logic. There was for them, first, a major division of the formal and nonformal logicians. The formal logicians were those for whom the subject-matter of thought was given; the given was to be made to fit into the formal modes of thought; in so far as it could not be made to do so, it was not proper subject-matter for logic. The adherents of this theory were the principal offenders for the idealists and Dewey, for whom the chief problem was the analysis of actual thought. Those who accepted this problem were the nonformal logicians. But these were subdivided into two groups, the empiricists and the idealists. The former held that thinking and proof proceeded inductively from given facts that were not gathered by thought. The idealists held to the transcendental logic that saw the universe as a construction of thought, constituted by reason, and they looked upon the logical process as a coming to consciousness of the rational structure possessed by the universe.[5] White declares that "the net result of this feverish drawing of lines and making of alliances was to show that the worst thing one could do was to be a formal logician, the next worst thing one could be was an inductive logician, and the thing one had to be was an idealist logician." [6] It is from this background of thought that Dewey developed the ideas which finally resulted in his opposition to all of these positions. These ideas begin to emerge in his first papers on logic in the 1890's.

IDEALIST OPPOSITION TO FORMAL LOGIC AND EMPIRICISM

Dewey accepted the problem of what he calls the Newer Logic which was, he says, "an attempt to take account of the newer methods of thinking employed by science, that is, of the methods the aim of which is truth, and which deal with a material of fact." [7] In recognizing this as the problem of logic, he dismisses formal logic in short order as unworthy of extended argument.[8] The Newer Logic

contrasts with the old scholastic logic, which may be roughly described as an attempt to deal with thinking *in vacuo,* that is with methods which leave out (or abstract from) the material of fact, and which have no aim except non-contradiction of their own premises—self-consistency. We may call the latter the logic of

argument, not of truth; but the former is the logic of science, i.e., of actual knowledge.[9]

But nonformal views on logic deserve more consideration, and the remainder of his discussion in this paper is a statement of Venn's position in a book called *Empirical Logic,* and of Dewey's differences with it. Venn's thesis is, "We must take for granted a duality. On the one hand, outside of us, there is the world of phenomena, pursuing its course; and on the other hand, within us, there is the observing and thinking mind. Logic is concerned with judgments of the latter about the former."[10] Dewey believes this means for Venn "internal thought" and "external things" as independent and separate data with logic as a third thing necessary to bring one to bear on the other. This is a case, though Dewey doesn't use the expression here, of getting the cart before the horse. "The duality between the object perceived and the thought conceived is not one with which the logical process begins, but is the result of the logical process; that is in so far as logic has anything to do with it."[11] And Dewey even calls upon Venn for support of his point. For the latter himself attacked the notion that "objects" were in a way marked out by nature, the same for all beings. Venn agreed that a considerable process of analysis and synthesis is involved in distinguishing objects. But, for him, the process did not fall within the scope of logic. Here is the main point of contention between Venn and Dewey— the question of the true province of logic. For Dewey argues: "Now it seems to me that as soon as we give up the view that objects are presented to the mind already distinguished from others and united into cohering wholes, we are tacitly admitting that logical processes enter into the recognition, or observation of facts."[12] He goes on to show that Venn would surely admit that analysis and synthesis are logical processes, for he classifies these as subdivisions of the process of framing hypotheses and suppositions. This line of argument leads Dewey to the conclusion that our first perceptions of objects are in a

sense tentative hypotheses. Now this is a startling statement
from a common sense point of view, for surely in ordinary
experience that "the fire burns" is a fact, not a supposition. But
Dewey points out that if "the sun moves" is substituted for
"the fire burns," the hypothetical nature of the ordinary perception is more obvious.

Thus Dewey takes a stand here that he maintained through
his later writings on logic. "Ordinary perception and scientific
reflection have just the same material, and follow, in the rough,
the same methods." [13] If we recall from our discussion of
Dewey's psychology the importance attached to the idea of
conflict and how ordinary experience develops through problem-solving situations, we can observe that the constitution of
problems and their resolution are the subject-matter of both
common sense and science, in which essentially the same logical processes are used. The difference between the two Dewey
here ascribes to the fact that they are unconsciously used in
ordinary experience, but consciously pursued in scientific reflection. [14] We have, then, this summation of Dewey's position:

There is but one world, the world of knowledge, not two, an
inner and an outer, a world of observation and a world of conception; and this one world is everywhere logical. As the world
of ordinary perception it is logical, but its logical character is
undeveloped, is latent, and hence is utilized at random, that is to
say, extravagantly and erroneously. As the world of scientific reflection, it is more completely logical, because its logical character
is brought to consciousness, it is rendered explicit, and is thus
used as a criterion, or a standard, in a word, as the truth by which
the false and the irrelevant may be excluded. The result is that
logic has no dualistic basis. [15]

When Dewey here says that there is one world everywhere
logical he is using typical idealist language. Ordinarily, this
language was used to convey the idea of the logical character
of what he, at the time, called universal consciousness. A
logical world was available for individual consciousness to

make out, but due to the latter's finiteness it could only partially realize this universal consciousness. However, perhaps a greater part could be made out by man if he had an adequate account of actual thought as exemplified by science. But neither formal nor empirical logic would achieve this since they both excluded thought from sharing in gathering its materials. Actual thought, Dewey argues, originates with the individual's encounters with the phenomenal world and guides, however erroneously and irrelevantly, his first stumbling perceptions. Thus both perception and conception as well as both common sense and science have a logical character. Here is one world everywhere logical in a different sense. And in the present context it seems to be more this sense that Dewey is emphasizing than the usual idealist sense of a logical world. He continues to hold this meaning while he later drops both the idealist meaning and idealist language. But at this point in his development he seems to mean both that the province of logic should be extended and that this would make it possible for individual consciousness better to arrive at the logical world of universal consciousness. Yet it is possible to foresee how the same evolutionary theory that influenced Dewey's psychology might change this sense of "arriving" to one of "making" where the conscious use of the logical processes can be instrumental in the formulation and solution of man's problems.

Obviously, if there is no world of observation or perception on one hand, and one of conception on the other, there must be a close relationship of perception and conception. This connection is more fully developed by Dewey in his paper "How Do Concepts Arise from Percepts?" To begin with, a concept is not a mental state but a function of a mental state which, as bare existence, is an image. As an image, the mental state is a particular and the nominalist is correct in saying there is no such thing as a general idea, if he is speaking of mental existences.[16] This particular mental image is the percept, while "The concept is the *power* which a particular image has of standing for or conveying a certain meaning or intellectual value. . . . The concept is something which the image does; some meaning which it conveys." [17] If we ask what meaning, Dewey answers: "The concept arises from the percept *through realizing the full meaning im*-plied, but not *ex*-plicit in the percept." [18] In any particular triangle for example, the principle that makes it a triangle and not something else, is implied.[19] When we get knowledge of this principle we have a concept, and the only way we get this concept is through the activity which constitutes it; this activity is one of construction; that is, to know the principle underlying any particular triangle is to know how it came to be or how it was constructed.

The concept in short, is knowledge of what the real object is— the object taken with reference to its principle of construction; while the percept, so called, is knowledge of the object in a more or less accidental or limited way. As to their intellectual value, concept means complete knowledge of an object—knowledge of it in its mode of genesis and in its relations and bearings; while percept means incomplete . . . knowledge of an object.[20]

The distinction between a concept and percept is not fixed, for the concept returns into and enriches the percept. Therefore ideally the concept and percept, if completely developed, would come to have the same content; and this is the ideal of every science.

Dewey uses this same theory of the reciprocal influence of conception and perception as the basis of verification of facts and ideas.[21] The distinction between fact and idea arises from disappointment of expectation. The disappointment creates need of adjustment and a consequent struggle among ideas. It is just the tentative holding of an idea that makes it an idea, while "the fact is the idea which nothing contradicts, which harmonizes with other ideas, which allows the mind free play and economical movement." [22] The process of transforming the tentatively held idea into a fact, or an idea held definitely, is verification. If we think of the original fact as one that did

not meet our expectations and the tentative idea as a hypothesis that will supply the need, we can say the hypothesis grows out of the fact but in turn alters the fact. "If the idea, the theory, is tentative, if it is pliable and must be bent to fit the facts, it should not be forgotten that the 'facts' are not rigid, but are elastic to the touch of the theory." [23] Another way to state the relationship is in terms of the particular and the universal. "The verification is the bringing together of this universal and particular; if the universal confronted with the particulars succeeds in filling out its own abstract or empty character by absorbing the particulars into itself as its own details, it is verified." And there is no other test of a theory than

its ability to *work*, to organize "facts" into itself as specifications of its own nature. But on the other side, the particulars attacked by the universal do not remain indifferent; through it they are placed in a new light, and as facts gain a new quality. . . . The important point is to see that verification is a two-edged sword." [24]

We have in the views Dewey expresses here a further emphasis on the notion of tension and conflict that we saw in his psychological theory. Even though there is more of a "mentalistic" tone expressed here, somewhat suggestive of Herbart, it is conflict whose resolution—which in a psychological sense brought good adjustment, "good" in that it freed activity for wider experiences—in the logical sense brings good hypotheses, "good" in that it allows the mind "free play and economical movement." Just as interest is not something externally attached to subject-matter but is an intrinsic part of a completed activity, so verification is internal to the logical process itself. Logic is not a form of thought used as a criterion for determining correspondence of idea and fact, nor to test coherence or consistency of ideas—ideas and facts which themselves are obtained outside the logical process. Rather, both fact and idea are determined by the logical process and their validity established within the process.

Dewey closes his writings on logic in this period with his paper "The Present Position of Logical Theory," which appeared in October, 1891.[25] Again he attacks formal logic and the conception of thought behind it, which, he says, is "that thought is a faculty or an entity existing in the mind, apart from facts, and that it has its own fixed forms, with which facts have nothing to do—except in so far as they pass under the yoke." [26] The continuation of the conception of formal logic is the last struggle of scholasticism to keep thought subject to authority.[27] He agrees that of the opposing logics, the "inductive" and the "transcendental," it is the former that has undermined the popularity of formal logic. Empirical logic is considered the logic of science; it does take account of experience. So it gains favor with Dewey, who says:

Whatever the defects of Locke's or Mill's account of experience, any theory which somehow presupposes a firsthand contact of mind and fact (though it be only in isolated, atomic sensations) is surely preferable to a theory which falls back on tradition, or on the delivery of dogma irresponsible to any intellectual criticism.

Nevertheless it is still inadequate logic, for

in its account of the derivation of the material of judgment, inductive logic is still hampered by the scholastic conception of thought. Thought, being confined to the rigid framework in which the material is manipulated after being obtained, is excluded from all share in gathering the material. The result is that this material, having no intrinsic thought-side, shrinks into a more or less accidental association of more or less shifting and transitory mental states.[28]

What is left to support is transcendental, idealist logic. This Dewey does: "Types of thought are simply the various forms which reality progressively takes as it is progressively mastered as to its meaning, that is, understood. Methods of thought are simply the various active attitudes into which intelligence puts itself in order to detect and grasp the fact." [29] Here is still the sense of individual consciousness "arriving" at the universal

consciousness. But he is obviously halfhearted. Phrases such as these appear: "If this is a fair description," "I shall not attempt any defence of the 'transcendental' logic," "simply taking this view of 'transcendental' logic for granted." He admits that "transcendental" logic is usually considered the especial foe of science, and it was the methods of science that he wanted to understand, not combat. What Dewey opposed at this time is clear enough; what he stood for is not; that he was dissatisfied is evident. This dissatisfaction undoubtedly stimulated and sustained his thinking on the problem of logic and resulted in his resolution of the difficulty, a solution made known in 1900 in his paper "Some Stages of Logical Thought."

FROM TRANSCENDENTAL TO EXPERIMENTAL LOGIC

The shift in Dewey's thinking does not represent a complete rejection of all his former ideas. He could continue to hold such views of the percept, concept, and verification that he used in his idealist attack on specific features of formal and empirical logic. But he has reinterpreted their meaning and place within an inclusive theory of logic that does break sharply with transcendental logic. He states the position at which he has arrived in the form of a question at the close of the paper:

Does not an account or theory of thinking, basing itself on modern scientific procedure, demand a statement in which all the distinctions and terms of thought—judgment, concept, inference, subject, predicate and copula of judgment, etc. ad *indefinitum*,— shall be interpreted simply and entirely as distinctive functions or divisions of labor within the doubt-inquiry process? [30]

To adopt this view means to abandon the three rival doctrines of logic, the formal, the empirical, and the transcendental. He repeats his familiar objections to the first two but his attack now upon transcendental logic, at least possibly to be anticipated from his earlier papers, is made explicit. For it is clear now to Dewey that for the transcendentalist

> Thought in itself is so far from a process of doubt or inquiry that it is the eternal, fixed structure of the universe; *our* thinking, involving doubt and investigation, is due wholly to our "finite," imperfect character, which condemns us to the task of merely imitating and reinstating "thought" in itself, once and forever complete, ready-made, fixed. It is per accidens an object of inquiry, but not its organic content.[31]

Thus Dewey rejects his former belief that the world is logical through and through in the idealist sense; he no longer explains the inadequacy of thought as being due to the finite character of men, which makes it impossible for them fully to realize the logic of ideas in the universal consciousness, as absolute. Instead, he sees life as precarious and uncertain, full of doubt and conflict. Thought is an instrument for guiding man to his advantage in confusing situations, and the fact that it may not function desirably is due, he now believes, to the social conditions which separate thought from its true function of guiding an active, emotional being in his relations with the physical and social world in which he lives.

So much for Dewey's relations with the current systems of logic. None of them is adequate; none accounts for the procedure of thought that occurs in modern science or in ordinary experience. Thought is a doubt-inquiry process conducted for the purpose of attaining that mental equilibrium known as assurance or knowledge. The relationship between assurance and doubt passes through several stages which it is Dewey's purpose to describe.

> I wish to show how a variety of modes of thinking, easily recognizable in the progress of both the race and the individual, may be identified and arranged as successive species of the relationship which doubting bears to assurance.[32]

Note that it is both the individual and the race that progresses through the stages of thought. Again we have the notion of

conflict and tension both within the individual and in his social relations. For when the object of assurance loses stable equilibrium, tension increases until a readjustment can be made.

The first of the four stages of thought is one where ideas are treated as something fixed or static. Words become attached to these ideas, but it is not the words that are responsible for the fixation of the idea but rather social usage. "The fixed or static idea is a fact as expressing an established social attitude, a custom." [33] There does develop in this stage a certain degree of discrimination or doubt, but it is simply involved in seeking from among a collection of ideas just the one to be used. Adults help the young by instructions to be prepared to choose correctly so that advances made by society will be perpetuated. Such instructions, rather than training in ability to think, train for escape from thinking; thus the fixation of ideas is abetted by instruction.

In this stage there are emergencies and crises;[34] there is a growing stock of fixed ideas whose application becomes more difficult, prolonged, and roundabout.

Critical cases come up in which the fiction of an idea or rule cannot be maintained. It is impossible to conceal that old ideas have to be radically modified before the situation can be dealt with. The friction of circumstance melts away their congealed fixity. Judgment becomes legislative.[35]

This questioning of formerly static ideas gives rise to the second stage of thought.[36] Now ideas are "batted about," their rigidity is shaken; the keynote is discussion, a conversation of thought. Out of this is generated logical theory in this interesting manner:

No process is more recurrent in history than the transfer of operations first carried on between different persons, into the arena of the individual's own consciousness. The discussion which at first took place by bringing ideas from different persons into contact, by introducing them into the forum of competition and by subjecting them to critical comparison and selective decision,

finally became a habit of the individual with himself. He became
a miniature social assemblage, in which pros and cons were
brought into play struggling for the mastery for final conclusion.
In some such way we conceive reflection to be born.[37]

Reflection thus germinated contributes to the reaction that
sets in against this agitation of ideas and the consequent dis-
crediting of all thinking.[38] This movement, the third stage,
"was concerned rather with the virtual appeal to a common
denominator involved in bringing different ideas into relation
with one another." [39] Discussion, besides extending doubt, also
involves appeal to a single thought acceptable to all. There are
really two parts to this stage, reasoning and methods of proof.
Socrates and Plato exemplify the search for higher ideas to
substantiate the lower; this search was conducted by reason.
Aristotle systematized methods by which general truths may
be employed to justify propositions otherwise doubtful; this
was the transformation of subjective reflection into proof.
The evolution of the doubt-inquiry function has arrived at
this state:

As compared with the period of fixed ideas, doubt is awake, and
inquiry is active but in itself, it is rigidly limited. On one side it is
bound by fixed ultimate truths, whose very nature is that they
cannot be doubted, that they are not products or functions in inquiry, but bases that investigation hits upon. In the other direction
doubt is itself arrested. All "matters of fact," all "empirical truths"
belong to a particular sphere or kind of existence, and one
intrinsically open to suspicion. The region is condemned in a
wholesale way. It itself exhales doubt; it cannot be reformed; it
is to be shunned, or, if this is not possible, to be escaped from
by climbing up a ladder of intermediate terms until we lay hold
on the universal.[40]

In Aristotle's time there were but few first principles; nor
were many necessary because the majority of values were still
carried by custom, religious belief, and social institutions. But

by the mediaeval period customs were dissipated through their mutual clash and Authority found it necessary to enlarge the sphere of first principles by intuition or revelation. But this same need for extension of the universals also created doubt and inquiry in the region of the particulars. So the fourth, or scientific, stage of thought is reached. Thought now takes the form of inference instead of proof.

It aims at pushing out the frontiers of knowledge, not with marking those already attained with signposts. Its technique is not a scheme for assigning status to ideas already possessed, but a method for making friends with facts and ideas hitherto alien. Inference reaches out, fills in gaps. Its work is measured not by the patents of standing it issues, but by the material increments of knowledge it yields. *Inventio* is more important than *judicium,* discovery than "proof." [41]

Instruments of research become organs of thinking; interest is in exceptions, in the discrepant; search is made for facts incompatible that might suggest new points of view. "Thinking consists in the extension and control of contact with new material so as to lead regularly to the development of new experience." [42] The four stages of thought, the doubt-inquiry process, are identified by the amount of play they give to doubt and the sincerity with which thinking is identified with free inquiry. Modern science seems to be the ideal in this development, although it has not yet "reflected itself into coherent and generally accepted theory of thinking." [43]

The four stages of thought, as we have seen, belong to the history of the race and of the individual. They are also steps in any given inquiry, as we learn in *Studies in Logical Theory.*[44] We have the dawning of a problem out of the original stage where facts and relations are taken for granted; then comes an empirical search for raw material, followed by the speculative stage, a period of guessing and making hypotheses; finally we have a period of fruitful interaction between ideas and facts, a period when observation is determined by experimental conditions depending upon the use of certain guiding conceptions; when reflection is directed and checked at every point by the use of experimental data, and by the necessity of finding such a form for itself as will enable it to serve in a deduction leading to evolution of new meanings, and ultimately to experimental inquiry which brings to light new facts.[45]

This is the final stage of inquiry and the highest level of thought reached by the race, either in ordinary experience or in scientific reflection. The continuity we have previously noted is here reemphasized:

Neither the plain man nor the scientific inquirer is aware as he engages in his reflective activity, of any transition from one sphere of existence to another. He knows no two fixed worlds—reality on one side and mere subjective ideas on the other; he is aware of no gulf to cross. He assumes uninterrupted free and fluid passage from ordinary experience to abstract thinking, from thought to fact, from things to theories and back again. Observation passes into development of hypotheses; deductive methods pass into use in description of the particular; inference passes into action, with no sense of difficulty save those found in the particular task in question. The fundamental assumption is *continuity* in and of experience.[46]

We may want to ask what difference this analysis of thought makes; how important is it to know what our present methods are? If we are now in the fourth and highest stage, we are there and let's continue without undue concern or reflection on reflection. If we ask, we find an interesting answer by Dewey, one that shows the importance of logic and also serves to indicate his ultimate concern:

Much of the immediate business of life is badly done because we do not know in relation to its congeners the organic genesis and outcome of the work that occupies us. The manner and degree of appropriation of the values achieved in various departments of social interest and vocation are partial and faulty because

we are not clear as to the due rights and responsibilities of one function of experience in reference to others.

The value of research for social progress; the bearing of psychology upon educational procedure; the mutual relations of fine and industrial art; the question of the extent and nature of specialization in science in comparison with the claims of applied science; the adjustment of religious aspirations to scientific statements; the justification of a refined culture for a few in face of economic insufficiency for the mass—such are a few of the many social questions whose final answer depends upon the possession and use of a general logic of experience as a method of inquiry and interpretation.[47]

A proper conception of logic as the history of the stages of thought is to help solve social questions. No claim is made that the only requirement is an adequate logic, nor is it said that progress cannot be made without it. But with it, progress will be less impeded and irregular; with it, we can criticize and organize tools of research; with it, it can further clarify its own problem, "the genesis and functioning in experience of various typical interests and occupations with reference to one another."[48]

SOME IMPLICATIONS FOR EDUCATION

Suppose, as is usually accepted in a democratic society, that one of the outcomes expected of an educational program is improved quality of thought. Consider, then, what the holding of different versions of the nature and scope of logic might imply for the method and subject-matter used to attain this end. While implications might well be sought in other directions also, perhaps this focus will add some measure of clarity to the meaning and significance of Dewey's position on logic.

It may be held that thought can be disciplined adequately and sufficiently through the use of the canons of formal logic. In this case, it would seem to follow that educational method

would provide the student with many opportunities to manip-
ulate and order subject-matter according to these rules. This
subject-matter could be presented to the student as given
material. He would practice arranging these data into the
formal modes of thought until he became conscious of the
rules and adept in their application. What subject-matter was
used would seem to make little difference, so far as this logic
itself would suggest. One criterion for the selection of material,
perhaps, might be that of relative difficulty and feasibility for
logical arrangement. Thus the content would proceed from
that which can be ordered by simple modes of thought to
that which necessitates use of the more complex forms. The
test to determine whether the end of improved quality of
thought is reached might be the mental agility shown in
ordering the material of thought in such expressions as argu-
mentation and debate.

If empirical logic is taken as the guide for educational method
and subject-matter designed to improve the quality of thought,
then, as with formal logic, it apparently suggests the presentation to the student of ready-made, given data for thought. But
instead of the student being led to order this material by the
rules of formal logic, he would be helped through successive
experiences with the data to arrive at generalizations, the concepts of thought. It seems that there would be less emphasis on
the mental functions in manipulating data abstracted from
concrete situations of life. Empirical logic purported to be an
account of actual thought in experience. It was a logic of
experience, the best use of which was to be found in science.
It seems to follow, then, that relatively more emphasis would
be placed upon the subject-matter for thought to be drawn from
actual experience. And, if science was the best example, then
the data and generalizations of this thought would seem to
be the ideal subject-matter. The more data presented, the more
with which thought would have to work. But all data available
could not be presented to the student; there would have to be

selection. As with formal logic, one criterion might be the
relative difficulty of the material and its feasibility, in this
case, for generalization. But beyond this, and the fact that
the material for thought is to come from concrete experience
and preferably in firsthand experiences, the logic itself seems
to point to no other significant criteria for selection. These, it
seems, would have to come from some source outside the
logic.

Dewey's theory of logic, like that of the empiricists, points
to education as experience and emphasizes the content of
experience rather than the mere forms of thought to which
this data is to be made to conform. But here the resemblance
ends, for the content of experience is not a ready-made, given
set of data. Thought begins with the individual in confused,
uncertain situations, where the meaning of immediate experience is in doubt. Such situations are precarious to the
individual's advantage, and he initiates inquiry by discrim-
inating and selecting elements of the situation and formulating
them into problems and tentative hypotheses for solutions.
Hence, education begins, not with given products of experience, but with the process of experiencing. As the immature
child engages in his on-going concerns, he encounters difficulties which check his activities, and thought arises as an
instrument for dealing with the obstacles so that he may
continue in the line of his interest.

The quality of thought used may lead only to temporary
freeing of the individual for the immediate furtherance of
his concerns, after which he may encounter new difficulties
which can be insurmountable. Or it may be such as to free
the individual so that, while new difficulties always arise, a
growing mind, including adequate methods of inquiry, can
resolve confusing situations to the individual's advantage. The
most adequate method is the experimental method of science,
and teachers must guide the child's process of experiencing
by leading him to the understanding and use of this method.

To share in the development of the child's thought, then, the school must provide the conditions for his participation in active concerns with which he identifies himself and which lend themselves most fruitfully to scientific inquiry for their satisfying continuation. The pursuits of occupations have both the required hold on the child's concerns and represent the area of life activities which best reflects the progressive development of the scientific method of inquiry.

Thought not only arises and is sustained by involvement of individuals in the on-going concerns and activities of living, but it functions in the mediation of this involvement with the physical and social world. That is, thought is always directed toward some object or content and is instrumental in relating this content with the individual's impulses, desires, and purposes. The principle for the selection of subject-matter, then, rests in the interpretation of the material which, at any moment, will best relate past experiences to new ones of expanding content. Just as occupations reflect the best use of the methods of science, they also represent not only a close and continuous relationship among themselves but also a core of dominant content of experiences to which all other objects of concern are ultimately tied. Thought and its data may, at any point in the process of living, be remote from immediate advantage and satisfaction, but it is meaningful and effective in the degree to which it is related to the basic concerns which must be fulfilled if the individual is to be at home in a limited world.[49]

In addition to the fact that Dewey's logic points to the development of thought through the process of experiencing in problem-solving situations encompassing the typical interests of man, a most significant implication of his theory stems from his view of the social nature of thought. We have noted the sense in which the individual becomes a "miniature social assemblage" through the transfer into his own consciousness of the operations first carried on between different persons. The

immature child participates in the interchange of experiences with other children and adults. At first he depends heavily upon adults to help him meet conflicts and overcome obstacles. Thought arises as he is forced to see and choose from among appropriate adult responses to particular situations. Later, if these responses do not further his interests, thought expands to dealing with doubts which arise because of their inadequacy. This extends the area of conflict and thought reaches out in speculative efforts to mediate his experiences with those of others, finally extending to the experimental testing of possible solutions.

Thus thought not only arises in social situations, but it is sustained and functions as the individual shares in common enterprises with others. As he communicates the meaning of his experiences to others and in return becomes conscious of their ideas and purposes, the resultant doubt and conflict force comparison, selection, and reformulation of ideas and meanings. Therefore, the development of thought is a social process and improvement of its quality must be sought in a social setting which encourages free communication and interchange of ideas. Since all ideas are directed toward some content, the sharing of them depends upon their mutual relatedness to a common content and concern. Thus the social setting for education must adhere to the principle of community, where individuals are held together by common purposes. And further, since the function of thought is instrumental to action, its adequacy must be tested in the community principle of not only purposing, but fulfilling purposes, of doing something. Thus education through community of effort enables thought to be completed as it passes over into action.

· IV ·

ETHICS

IN ORDER to appreciate the problem of ethics with which Dewey was concerned, it is well to observe, first, the difficulties he saw in the current ethical theories. As will be seen, the two general weaknesses of these theories are their neglect of the best method of thought—science—and their failure to support an adequate conception of democracy. The grounds for these objections will emerge from a brief review of each of the four ethical views which Dewey criticizes.

Hedonism

One doctrine of ethics, hedonism, is based upon a psychology that explains action as being motivated from passive states of feeling; the individual is moved to act by feelings of pleasure. It is obvious that Dewey could not accept this psychology. We know that for him, activity begins with impulse; consciousness of the impulse becomes desire; and desire becomes motive only when the end and its means of attainment become identified. But Dewey's difficulty with hedonism stems not alone from differences in psychologies; even more disturbing is the fact that ethical judgments must ignore motives. For, he says, if the hedonistic theory of motivation were correct, "that the individual should not be moved by pleasure, and what, at the time of acting, is the greatest possible pleasure, would be a psychological impossibility," and, therefore, "every motive would be good, or rather there would be no distinction of good or bad pertaining to the motive." [1]

We come then, to the hedonistic criterion for the moral act. This also depends upon a passive state of feeling, and again,

it must be one of pleasure. The moral act is that which brings a feeling of pleasure to the agent. This end bears no relationship to the motive or means of attainment. Again, it is obvious that Dewey could not accept this separation of means and ends. Furthermore, as he saw it, passive states of feeling could not be used as a standard for the rightness of acts, for each act would result in a distinct state of feeling, independent of all others. The reliance on static conditions instead of on a developing process affords no unifying principle that can guide the making of a moral life. More important, not only is the individual's life left as a series of isolated, disconnected acts, but there is the same lack of workable standard for social conduct. Dewey argues that, for hedonism,

The end for each man is his own pleasure. Pleasure is nothing objective in which men may equally participate. It is purely individual in the most exclusive sense of that term. It is a state of feeling and can be enjoyed only while felt, and only by the one who feels it. To set it up as the ideal of conduct is to turn life into an exclusive and excluding struggle for possession of the means of personal adjustment; it is to erect into a principle the idea of war of all against all.[2]

Utilitarianism

A second type of ethical theory, utilitarianism, attempts to supply the hedonistic theory with a more adequate criterion for the moral act. Based upon the same psychology, and accepting pleasure as the end of action, it provides a general, as distinct from a private, end. The standard of conduct for the utilitarians is not the individual's own pleasure but the greatest amount of happiness for all together, or, more popularly, the greatest good of the greatest number. But, Dewey argues, if the utilitarians accept individual pleasure as the driving force, "how do we get from individual pleasure to the happiness of all?"[3] The intuitionist says it is a self-evident principle that one is morally bound to regard the welfare of others. But this makes general welfare or happiness a mere abstraction, when it is actually a particular condition of a concrete person. The empiricist says that each person's good is a good to him, and, therefore, that general happiness is a good to an aggregate of persons. But this is illogical, Dewey says:

Because all men want to be happy, it hardly follows that every man wants all to be happy. There is accordingly no *direct* road from individualistic hedonism—private pleasure—to universalistic —general pleasure.

Furthermore, the psychology is still faulty:

Moreover, if we adopt the usual psychology of hedonism and say that pleasure is the motive of acting, it is absolutely absurd to say that general happiness can be a motive. How can I be moved by the happiness that exists in someone else? I may feel a pleasure resembling his, and be moved by it, but that is quite a different matter.[4]

When the utilitarians attempt to chart an *indirect* road between private and public happiness by means of sympathetic and social emotions, and through education and law, Dewey replies that such relationship is always extrinsic and therefore open to inexplainable exception. Besides, it presupposes an ideal of identity of personal and general happiness and does not explain how the general welfare becomes an end for the individual. He claims that this position is logically untenable:

Instead of the essentially vague idea of states of pleasurable sensation we have the conception of a community of interests and ends, in securing which alone is true happiness to be found. This conception of the moral ideal we regard as essentially true, but it is not hedonism. It gives up wholly the notion that pleasure is the *desired*, and since it sets up a standard by which it determines pleasure, it gives up equally the notion that pleasure as such is the desirable.[5]

Evolutionary Ethics

A third type of ethical theory is the attempt to combine utilitarian morality with the theory of evolution. Dewey credits this effort particularly to Herbert Spencer, who claims three advantages in using the evolutionary approach. It is more scientific in that it substitutes consideration of causes of the results of action for mere study of effects. It reconciles intuitionism and empiricism, for what we intuit is really the result of past experience which empirical method can give us. And lastly, it reconciles individual and general happiness, because the conditions of individual survival demand adjustment to what is largely a social environment. As Dewey puts it, "the conditions of survival demand altruistic action, and hence such action must become pleasurable to the agent (and in that sense egotistic)." [6]

Dewey's criticism should be obvious from the last statement; it may be true but it isn't hedonism. He says:

Spencer's hedonism in its final result hardly comes to more than saying that in case of a perfect individual in a perfect society, every action whatever would be accompanied by pleasure, and that therefore, *in such a society,* pleasure would be an infallible sign and test of the morality of action—a possibility which is not denied by any ethical writer whatever, unless a few extreme ascetics. [7]

Dewey stops his criticism at this point, after showing only that this attempt to combine the theory of evolution with hedonism tends rather to destroy the latter. He does make this comment, however, in discussing the effects of the idea of evolution making pleasure a test *after* society and the individual become perfect, or as he says, after activity becomes full and complete: "What is this but to admit . . . that activity itself is what man wants; not mere activity, but the

activity that belongs to man as man, and which therefore has
for its realized content all man's practical relationships." [8]

Formal Ethics

We have seen the effect of the theory of evolution on
Dewey's psychology and logic and might anticipate its effect
on his ethical theory. But before turning to the positive development of his own ethics, there is a fourth type, formal
ethics, to consider. The typical instance is Kantian ethics; it
is based on the same psychology as hedonism; pleasure is the
object of desire. But pleasure can give no universal end of
action. As Dewey had asked of hedonism, Kant considers how
we get from individual pleasure to the happiness of all. For
him, man's reason enables him to attach supreme value to the
ideal of social justice. Though individual pleasure may be
desired by man, his thought of this universal moral standard,
or law, supplies the motive for his actions. Reason, potentially
present in all men, may establish their allegiance to the moral
law. They are moral when motivated to conduct themselves
in conformity with its dictates. While hedonism determines
the moral act by its consequences, Kant finds rightness entirely in the motive. This, of course, is a separation which
Dewey rejects. If motive is divorced from desire, there is no
spring to action. When Kant allows one feeling to be rational,
that of reverence, he is wholly arbitrary. If, on the other hand,
motives are independent of consequences, the standard for
rightness of acts is a mere abstraction and offers no guide in
concrete situations. For this is what happens in formal ethics,
according to Dewey:

Each act must be considered independently of every other, and
must be capable of generalization on its own account. Each motive
of action must be capable of being *itself* a universal law of nature.
Each particular rule of action is thus made absolute, and we are
left not with one universal which comprehends all particulars

in their relations to one another, but literally with a lot of universals. These not only fail to have a unity, but each, as absolute, must contradict some other.[9]

However, Kant performed a positive service to the theory of ethics, a contribution whose description facilitates a transition from Dewey's criticism to his own position on ethics at the time. Dewey commends Kant for having a clear insight into the fact that the good is found only in activity whose end is the will—which Dewey translates into self-realization—and not some end external to self. And, too, Kant showed the necessity of curbing immediate impulse and subordinating it to some law not found in the particular desire. Of course, Kant erred in excluding desire from the moral motive, but he was right, Dewey thinks, in holding that desire must be controlled by universal law.

DEWEY'S EARLY ETHICS

Consistent with the first of Kant's insights, Dewey defines the moral end or good as the realization, by a person and as a person, of individuality. A person, we know, is active; he is capable of seeing ends and of attempting to realize them. But what is this individuality? There are two aspects, two sides, to individuality:

On the one side, it means special disposition, temperament, gifts, bent, or inclination; on the other side, it means special station, situation, limitations, surroundings, opportunities, etc. Or let us say, it means *specific capacity* and specific environment.[10]

This environment is not what is merely present in space, but the part of it that appeals to consciousness, that affects the make-up of an agent. Keeping this in mind, and with such a definition of individuality before us, we can restate the moral end as:

The performance by a person of his specific function, this function consisting in an activity which realizes wants and powers with reference to their peculiar surroundings.[11]

Since the individual's functions are specific, there can be no detailed statement of the content of moral ends; these are particular and concrete. But, since functions are active, objective, and satisfying interests, certain typical interests can be recognized. Dewey says these are:

Interests in persons and interest in things. And these may be subdivided: Interest in *self* and *others*. Interest in things—into their contemplation (knowledge) and into their production (art). And art again may be either productive of things to be contemplated (fine art), or useful—manufactures, industry, etc.[12]

For Dewey to say that the development of the typical interests is the moral end of life is to put himself in sharp opposition to several moral ideas of the time. Some argued that interest in self is to be selfish, and hence immoral; for Dewey, interest in self *may* take the form of selfishness if specific capacity is not expressed with reference to the full range of the specific environment. The fact is, however, that all conduct *must* arise from some interest on the part of an agent. Some contended that interest in others means giving up one's interest in self.[13] Others said that it is a disguised interest in the self. These positions separate egoistic and altruistic interests, while Dewey's definition of individuality provides that self-realization and social action are simply abstractions of the true relationship. But Dewey's greatest divergence from the standpoint of many is his insistence that interest in things, that is, interest in science and art, especially including useful arts, constitutes goodness in the same sense of devotion, say, to family or state. The usual view would see these interests as nonmoral or immoral, or, at best, they would be seen only as means to some ulterior moral end. But Dewey says that "moral goodness pertains to the kind of

idea or end which a man clings to, and not to what he happens to effect visibly in others." [14] Therefore, any artisan who "has his heart in his work," who holds to his best technical and artistic capacity, is realizing his capacity in a specific situation; and this meets the definition of the moral end.[15]

Thus Dewey locates the good for the individual within his activities as he seeks to fulfill, to complete, to realize, his typical interests; the good is in the process of functioning, not in mere results. But it is specific functioning and always with reference to the environmental situation; it is here that Dewey reconstructs Kant's universal law to which immediate impulse must be subordinated. We saw that, for Kant, acting out of regard for law as law was required of the individual by his own reason. But Dewey's definition of individuality includes adjustment and response to the needs of an environment which, taken in its fullness, is a community of persons. Thus,

Any law imposed by such a self would be "universal," but this universality would not be an isolated possession of the individual; it would be another name for the concrete social relationships which make the individual what he is, as a social member or organ. Furthermore, such a universal law would not be formal, but would have a content—these same relationships.[16]

Therefore the moral end that both unifies individual conduct and affords the common good can be termed synonymously "the realization of individuality," "the performance of specific functions," "the satisfaction of interests," or "the realization of a community of individuals." That the realization of individuality and the realization of community can be synonymous is Dewey's ethical postulate, which he states as follows:

In the realization of individuality there is found also the needed realization of some community of persons of which the individual is a member; and, conversely, the agent who duly satisfies the community in which he shares, by that same conduct satisfies himself.[17]

Thus Dewey arrives at what may be called the fundamentals of a democratic ethics. For the individual's good is achieved in social situations where his impulses are mediated in interaction with those of others, and these social relationships constitute his and the community's good. The relationship between the two basic ethical concepts of responsibility and freedom is clear; man is under obligation to perform his function as man; in the performance of this function, he finds his freedom.

This postulate rests upon faith so far as ethics is concerned. But it is not a blind faith, nor one made to fit the theory. It is a faith whose ultimate grounding is in metaphysics, and for Dewey at this time, in Hegelian metaphysics. We have seen the idealist sense in which for Dewey, originally, the world was logical through and through. Now we might also say that it is moral through and through. Ethical ideals are in the universal consciousness and are objectified in man's institutions, manners, and beliefs. But as individual consciousness strives to realize itself by getting in tune with these ideals, even it is aware that existing morality embodied in institutions often contradicts the ideal. But what is its method and basis for making this judgment? It is that reflective intelligence discloses the ideal already there, intended, but imperfectly embodied in existing institutional arrangements. The standard for ethical judgments, not ethical relationships, is available in the world. As man improves his methods for judging the contradictions by this standard, he can increasingly realize the ideals. Thus, morality can be progressive. Dewey reconciles an imperfect existing morality with an ethical world in the following idealistic explanation:

The existing moral status is never wholly self-consistent. It realizes ideals in one relation which it does not in another; it gives rights to "aristocrats" which it denies to the low-born; to men, which it refuses to women; it exempts the rich from obligation which it imposes upon the poor. Its institutions embody a common good

which turns out to be good only to a priviliged few, and thus existing in self-contradiction. They suggest ends which they execute only feebly or intermittently. Reflective intelligence cross-questions the existing morality; it extracts from it the ideal which it pretends to embody, and thus is able to criticise the existing morality in the light of its *own* ideal. It points out the inconsistencies, the incoherencies, the compromises, the failures, between the actual practice and the theory at the basis of this practice. And thus the new ideal proposed by the individual is not a product of his private opinions, but is the outcome of the ideal embodied in existing customs, ideas and institutions.[18]

To sum up Dewey's position as stated in the *Outlines of a Critical Theory of Ethics,* we recall that conduct begins with impulse; both motive and end arise in the process of realizing the impulse—in the course of the performance of functions in a situation; the functions performed are the typical interests in persons and things; the criterion of performance, on the one hand, is the freedom of the expression of the impulse, but that this can be no individual, capricious, subjective end is denied by the fact that, on the other hand, the criterion of performance resides in meeting the situation, that is, it is subject to the universal law of a social environment. This law is objectified by its embodiment in institutions, or rather, in ideals that, through reflective intelligence, the individual becomes conscious of, as being intended by the institutions.

TRANSITION

But Dewey is obviously worried by the metaphysical foundations of his theory. In the same year that his *Outlines* appeared, 1891, he published a paper on "Moral Theory and Practice." In it, he says that he is considering the relation of moral theory to practice in order to clear up his own thinking. He denounces abstract moralizing and insists that "there is no such thing as conduct in general; conduct is what and where and when and how to the last inch." [19] Moral theory cannot be unrelated, extrinsic to conduct; it cannot exist in a book. "It is a piece of scholasticism to suppose that a moral rule has its own self-defining and self-applying content . . . it is only the breath of intelligence blowing through such rules that keeps them from the putrefaction which await all baren idealities." [20] So there must be a place for intelligence to guide conduct, but it still does so, for Dewey, at this time, only by grasping a cross-section view of the movement of history— "then intelligence removes its break, its abstracting hold, and the scene moves on." [21]

In two articles appearing in 1892 and 1893, which were devoted to an attack on Green, Dewey continues his search for an ethical theory that is part of conduct, not simply a judgment about it after the fact. In the first paper, he contends that Green merely substitutes, for Kant's dualism of reason and desire, a dualism of the unified self and the self in a particular act—that Green had not yet grasped the organic reality of experience, as had, say, Hegel.[22] But in the second paper, in discussing the meaning of self-realization, Dewey says:

The notion I wish to criticise is that of the self as a *presupposed, fixed schema* or outline, while realization consists in the filling up of this schema. The notion which I would suggest is that of the self as always a concrete *specific* activity; and, therefore (to anticipate) of the identity of self and realization.[23]

That is, realization is not the result of the self getting in step with the movement of ideals so that the individual finds his proper placement in accord with the evolution of the ideal. Such metaphysical ethics will not permit much headway, Dewey decides, against hedonistic and theological ethics that afford no assistance in particular experiences.[24] Ethics must be grounded in the self, and "the self must be conceived as a working, practical self, carrying within the rhythm of its own process both 'realized' and 'ideal' self. . . . The great need of

ethical theory today is a conception of the ideal as a working ideal—a conception which shall have the same value and which shall play the same part in ethics that the working hypothesis performs for the natural sciences." [25]

So it is that in the following year, 1894, in his *Study of Ethics: A Syllabus,* Dewey drops all references to Hegelian metaphysics because "the working man, of busy life, must have an ideal by which he can go into action, one which defines specific acts." Just as he, himself, had formerly done, "Green attempts to meet the need by reference to the past institutions in which the ideal is embodied. . . . But, since such embodiments are, according to him, only apparent, not real, it is difficult to see how this gives the required instructions." [26] Not only does the ideal pretended by institutions, or any other absolute or separate ideal, fail to give instruction, but also, "it makes a dualism, practically unbridgeable, between the moral and scientific phases of our experience." It is, then, concern for the function of science that bothers Dewey about the position stated in his *Outlines.* "If any account of the ideal can be given meeting the needs of the case, we should certainly hesitate before accepting a mode of statement introducing ideas which not only do not lie within the scope of scientific method as usually presented, but which emphasizes their complete *transcendence* of scientific categories and results." [27]

Dewey admits that moral science involves ideas that are not expressly brought out by physical or biological science; but he insists that ethics is a science with no sharp break between it and other sciences. For any object of any science arises from impulse and eventually reacts back into the impulse. The distinction to be made is merely that physical science deals with the *content* of mediation of the impulse, while moral science is concerned with the *process* of mediation. Physical science assumes the fact of value to the individual but it does not deal with the reasons for, or the nature of, the value its objects have for human experiences. But just because it doesn't consider these problems, it does not follow that physical science denies the fact of further conscious value.

It simply concentrates itself upon other aspects of reality—the *content* which gives value independent of how or why it gives it. Neglect is not denial of value; and recognition of value is not denial of science. Ethics completes the analysis of reality—experience—begun by physical and biological science.[28]

Thus Dewey's ethical postulate no longer rests upon faith sustained ultimately by metaphysics.[29] It is analogous with the scientific postulate of uniformity in nature and the reign of law. "That is, we demand order in our experience. The only proof is experimental."[30]

DEWEY'S RECONSTRUCTED ETHICS

Now that Dewey's theory has different foundations, it is advisable to review it as stated in the *Syllabus* in order that his newer position can be seen more clearly. His psychology has the same familiar base—the impulse. Impulses are not separate but interconnected tendencies. Each impulse in its expression tends to call up other impulses and brings to consciousness other experiences.

The expression of every impulse stimulates other experiences and these react into the original impulse and modify it. This reaction of induced experiences into the inducing impulse is the psychological basis of moral conduct.[31]

The back-reference of induced to inducing impulses, Dewey calls the mediation of impulse. This mediation idealizes and controls the impulse and this constitutes volition. It is this process that furnishes the check upon immediate desire that Kant sought in will and Dewey, formerly, in self-realization. The induced experiences, or consequences of the primary impulse, being referred back to it, *are* the moral and conscious act.

There are three degrees of completeness of the process of mediation. A complete reaction is habit; a less complete, yet still closely connected back-reference, gives us our more continuous and permanent expectations which form the framework of experience and keep us from caprice and the flux of circumstances; the third degree is one of particular, variable acts where the experiences which express the impulse are so numerous and so complex as to be uncertain. It is the conflict arising within the process of mediation of impulse, between habitual and variable factors, that constitutes the significance of our conduct morally. The way in which we mediate these impulses is character, while conduct is the expression of the mediation. Now, when is character "good" or conduct "right"?

The completest possible interaction of an impulse with all other experiences, or the completest possible relation of an impulse to the whole self constitutes the predicate, or moral value of an act.[32]

The criterion as well as the ideal is within the act and is the completest possible view of the act.

The original mediation of impulse is through the special consequences related to that special impulse. But as consequences develop, it is seen that they are not one lot of experience isolated from the whole system. It is seen that the consequence chief in importance is that upon the agent's own habits of action, his capacities, tastes, attitude toward life, ways of forming ends, etc.; in short, *the* consequence is the mediation, not of this or that impulse, but of the entire actual self. The mediation of the particular impulse has meaning only in relation to the placing or function of that impulse in the system of self—are thus one. The act is the subject; but *what* the act is—the predicate—is known only by placing the act, in its obvious features, in the right position in the whole activity. If we look at this whole activity as that which the agent is urging toward in every "act," it is Ideal; if we look at it as really deciding the nature and value of the "act" it is Criterion.[33]

Such a conception of criterion, Dewey believes, will realistically serve as a guide to conduct; it is workable. The agent always has his criterion with him; it is useful where an external criterion fails, in that the latter is not translatable into terms of particular, concrete situations. It is absolute in that all terms are within the act, yet relative in that it is flexible in variable cases. And we may say, though Dewey doesn't here, that it makes a place for science. He says, "Such a criterion, finally, requires acute and objective examination of the conditions of action, as the external criterion demands continued subjective introspection to see how far along we have got." [34] And, of course, methods of acute and objective examination mean science, science that helps moral life by freeing it, "by making it more significant and effective—as knowledge of mechanics helps a bridge builder." [35]

Thus, not only does a democratic ethics find a place for science, it calls upon science as a guide to moral living. We must recognize that this was quite shocking doctrine for many, perhaps especially for those whose practices prevailed in the schools. For the usual notion was that science had nothing to do with value; value was spiritual; it was something apart from, or above, science. So Dewey was concerned to establish the position of science as a method for morality in two articles published in 1902.[36] In these papers Dewey says that it is the historical or genetic method or group of ideas centering in the term evolution that is useful in the problem of morality. Science (here the term refers to the natural sciences) gives intellectual control; it analyzes any phenomena by showing the conditions of their coming into being and therefore is itself an historical or evolutionary method; then, why can't a similar genetic treatment of ethical ideas and practices yield control of conduct? It can, and in this manner:

The historic method is a method, first, for determining how specific moral values (whether in the way of customs, expectations, conceived ends, or rules) came to be; and second, for determining

their significance as indicated in their career. Its assumptions are
that norms and ideals, as well as unreflective customs, arose out of
certain situations, in response to the demands of those situations;
and that once in existence they operated with a less or greater
meed of success (to be determined by study of the concrete case).
We are still engaged in forming norms, in setting up ends, in con-
ceiving obligations. If moral science has any constructive value, it
must provide standpoints and working instrumentalities for the
more adequate performance of these tasks.[37]

When Dewey says here that moral science must provide
"standpoints," the place of historic method seems clear; but
when he also says it must provide "working instrumentalities,"
its function is not so obvious. Perhaps his thinking at this
point can best be traced by noting his comments on two
current methods of arriving at moral judgments—intuition
and empiricism. Intuitions, as self-evident, have no objective
validity, he argues, unless their genetic relationships to the
situations in which they appear can be shown; yet this is
declared unnecessary by the intuitionists. Not only do they
deny the reference necessary to validity, they cannot explain
the exceptions and variations of the contents of past intuitions,
and this is fatal to the method. "Either everything that appears
to the individual as final and authoritative is such, or else such
appearance lacks competency in any case." [38] Empiricism, he
holds, has been helpful in showing that many intuitions were
mere emotional sanctifications of custom, prejudice, factitious
association, and class interest. Nevertheless, the empirical
method is also open to criticism. The empirical theory, which
also excludes genetic considerations, holds that an idea arises
as a reflex of some existing object or fact; belief or idea is
generated by a process of repetition or cumulation; like elements pile up to reenforce each other, unlike ones fade. The
result is, according to Dewey:

If a moral belief is simply an accumulation through repeated associations of previously given elements of experience without any

essential modification or reconstruction of them, then one of two things is certain: either the original state was inherently ethical in quality—and thus the contention of the intuitionist is virtually admitted—or else the empiricist is trying to generate the ethical by telescoping into one another purely non-ethical elements. Here is the vulnerable point in empiricism—by its logic change of quality in passage from generating elements to final product must be explained away.[39]

Because of this, empiricism can only be critical, destructive; it can offer no direction, no selection, no "working instrumentalities," and since it tends to destroy even the best of working ideals, it inevitably brings intuitionism to the rescue of the ideal. It is the weakness of these methods that suggests the importance of historic method:

To help us see the present situation comprehensively, analytically, to put in our hands a grasp of the factors that have counted, this way or that, in the moralizing of man, that is what the historic method does for us. If our moral judgments were just judgments *about* morality, this might be of scientific worth, but would lack moral significance, moral helpfulness. But moral judgments are judgments of ways to act, of deeds to do, of habits to form, of ends to cultivate. Whatever modifies the judgment, the connection, the interpretation, the criterion, modifies conduct. To control our judgments of conduct, our estimates of habit, deed, purpose, is in so far forth to direct conduct itself.[40]

Again we have the notion that historical method gives us perspective; it helps us see "the factors that have counted." But science can also serve to control judgments, and just as our beliefs about the physical world have been controlled and our activities affected by experimental science, so, Dewey comes to believe, it is experimental science which can modify our judgments of conduct and serve to control our deeds and purposes. That is, he comes to expect historical method to provide the "standpoint," experimental science to provide the "working instrumentalities." He defends his point of view in

1903 in "Logical Conditions of a Scientific Treatment of Morality." [41] In this paper, he says that objections to his view that moral judgments can be reached by the scientific method can be reduced to the claim that scientific statements refer to generic conditions, which are capable of complete and objective statement, while ethical judgments refer to individual acts which transcend objective statement. He seeks to show that scientific generalizations *do* take account of particular acts. Scientific judgments arise, and are developed and employed for the purpose of freeing and reenforcing acts of judgment that apply to individual cases. And, on the other hand, ethical judgments in particular cases rely for their control on generic propositions.

Dewey summarizes the net import of his discussion in this article thus:

The whole discussion implies that the determination of objects as objects, even when involving no conscious reference whatever to conduct, is, after all, for the sake of the development of further experience. Thus further development is change, transformation of existing experience, and thus is *active*. So far as this development is intentionally directed through the construction of objects as objects, there is not only active experience, but *regulated activity*, i.e., conduct, behavior, practice. [42]

Now this "transformation of existing experience" and "the construction of objects as objects" indicates, not historic, but experimental, phase of method. It is experimental science which he now sees as instrumental to this task; for if moral science is to be constructive, it must provide such a working instrument.

Here then is finally seen the formulation of the relationships between democracy and science in ethics—the relationships he originally saw as unexplained by the current ethical theories. It is historical method which builds the democratic standpoint; it is the democratic view which interprets the disclosures of this method as support for the democratic standpoint. These mutually supporting factors provide the perspective, the ethical character and habits, from which experimental science is launched as an instrument to further the development of ethical judgments and practices.

SOME IMPLICATIONS FOR EDUCATION

At the time Dewey was formulating his ethical theory, there was a growing emphasis upon the place of moral training in the school. The trend was to add attention to moral development onto the usual intellectual training; this implied a separation of the two and tended to reflect the divisions set by hedonistic and formal ethics. We have seen that for hedonism, an act is to be judged by its consequences, apart from the motive, and apart from the quality of the process, either emotional or intellectual, through which the consequences resulted. In formal ethics an act is to be judged by the motive of the agent; again, the motive is apart from consequences and the quality of the processes through which it is developed.

The implication of either view seems to be that moral training is something appended to the still dominant intellectual aspect of schooling. Either the student's work and life in the school must start with right motives or must conclude with right results. The quality of the life and work itself would not appear so important. There is, apparently, no functioning guide to desirable processes in successive situations developing the motive, or leading to conclusive consequences.

While hedonism and formal ethics are similar in implying this separation of moral from emotional and intellectual training, they differ in the methods they suggest for attaining moral development. If we look to motive, as in formal ethics, it would seem necessary to strengthen the will to act in accord with law instead of immediate desire. Until such time as the individual is able to will such a will for himself, he must be curbed in the expression of his desires and exhorted to ap-

preciate moral precepts.[43] On the other hand, if we look to consequences, as in hedonism, it would probably be useful to reward the individual for good results and punish him for undesirable outcomes.[44]

The two current methods of selecting good motives and interpreting good consequences were the intuitive and empirical. The intuitive method is more than a mere hunch that one motive is better than another. This conclusion is reached by a careful process of reasoning from first principles that are seen with utter clarity and certainty. Until the immature mind is capable of this type of reasoning, reliance would likely be placed upon the teacher for the selection of proper motives. Thus, authoritarian edict would determine the individual's approach to conduct. If, as may happen, different teachers start from different intuitions, or if, when his powers develop, the individual's own intuitions and process of reason lead him to different motives, the resultant conflict would be apt to leave him in moral confusion.

The empirical method has shown that if this contradiction does not develop the tendency will be to sanctify the existing morality. For this method sees moral ideas as reflexes generated from an accumulation of repeated experiences. As often happens, this method brings evidence to bear that subsequent consequences in experience have resulted in discarding earlier moral beliefs derived from the intuitive method. While it thus undermines one method of selecting moral ideas, it, too, tends to sanctify the status quo, for it arrives at the position of accepting the currently dominant beliefs as the right ones. Thus it serves to judge consequences by authoritarian edict. Again, if the immature child is exposed to ideas reflecting current experiences which differ from those of the authorities in school, or if his later experiences reflect new ideas that contradict the old, the individual could easily be left in a state of confusion, if not in moral skepticism.[45]

When we look to Dewey's ethical theory for its implications

for education, we can see the radical significance of his insistence that moral ideals must be working ideals, must be guides in specific situations, and, moreover, that the agent must have his ideal and criterion with him. Here is no separation of the moral and the intellectual; instead, intellectual development is instrumental in moral education. The individual must exercise his functions in full and free mediation with a primarily social situation if his expressions are to have desirable ethical quality. The requirements for this social setting are three. It must be a form of community life where all the members of the community participate fully and freely in common enterprises in which the special functions of each must be grounded. The common endeavors must be approached from the standpoint of humanity, a perspective built by engaging in the study and processes of historical method. And, the obligation of the school community to fulfill its purposes must be achieved through the "test and see" method of experimental science.

The first requirement demands that the school conditions and atmosphere be such as to permit and encourage full mediation of the impulses, the desires, and the interests of each member of the community with the experiences induced by others. The criterion for judging the ethical quality of this process of mediation is not merely whether the individual's motives are good, or his achievements acceptable as determined by authoritarian edict, but whether mediation of experience in each successive situation is complete enough to free the individual and the community of persons for further, growing experiences. In short, moral character is to be built through the process of living in a democratic community functioning in accord with the principle of free and intelligent participation in the sharing of experiences.

The second requirement demands that the school must focus on building the democratic perspective—on viewing from the standpoint of humanity. Historical method serves this function

as it discloses the relations, the evolution, and the development of all aspects of life, of useful production, of art, of knowledge, of spiritual ideals, out of the matrix of the typical, dominant interests of mankind—their occupations. Thus, the school is to bring ethical considerations to bear upon the everyday activities and callings of men. This area of life, which had been separated, from time long past, as a mere necessity to sustain the higher life of ideals and values, is to be made the focus of activities through which moral character is built. Historical method, by helping pupils see the significance and meaning of daily work and occupations in full relationship with man's highest ideals and purposes, will provide them with the perspective required to extend the ethical realm to serve as a guide in the everyday particular and concrete experiences of life.

The third requirement for the social setting is that the school must provide the community principle of doing something in and with the world, of planning and fulfilling purposes and ends. Ethical judgments are incomplete if they pertain only to motives or to consequences; they must focus upon the quality of purposing and the planning and creation of the fulfillment of the purposes. Occupations provide the conditions for relating means to ends through the instrumentality of thought, and for consummating goals and plans in action. In this responsibility to do, or make, to contribute something to the life of the community, rests the occasion for the building of moral character. The quality of the process of acceptance and furtherance of this responsibility, its grounding in the community enterprises and values, and its control by the method of experimental science is the focus of the community standard for ethical living.

· V ·

SOCIAL PHILOSOPHY

A STUDY of the papers Dewey published through the time of his experimental school reveals, as we have seen, an explicitly stated development of his ideas on psychology, on logic, and on ethics. But there is no similarly distinct and continuing series of articles that may be classified as a statement of his social philosophy. Yet even the casual reader knows that Dewey is often called the philosopher of democracy. That this, to a considerable extent, is due to his later twentieth-century writings may be true; but nevertheless his democratic faith is postulated in his earliest papers and there are constant references in all of his first articles that rest upon this premise. Dewey, of course, was quite a controversialist; when a writer's thinking led him astray he was apt to find Dewey, while honoring his ability to stir the thoughts of others, critically and carefully destroying his position. Psychologists, logicians, and moralists were particularly vulnerable; even social writers like Ward and Kidd, as we noted, were attacked more for their faulty psychology than for their social philosophy. That Dewey did not feel called upon to engage in controversy to defend his democracy is partly explained, perhaps, by a statement he makes in "Ethics and Physical Science," which appeared in 1887.

DEMOCRACY AS AN END

This paper itself is one of Dewey's early idealistic attacks on empiricism and the notion that physical science could formulate a constructive ethics. His arguments on this point are not our concern in the present context; rather, a statement that he includes in his discussion is of pertinent interest. It

shows that he did not feel it necessary to fight for and defend a democratic thesis simply because, whether they knew it or not and whether they built properly from it or not, all schools accepted the same faith.

However much ethical schools differ theoretically, they are practically agreed on one point; the universality of the moral end, in the sense that it is applicable to all who come under it. The intuitionist, like Lotze, who makes benevolence itself the final end; the utilitarian, whose formulae are the "greatest happiness of the greatest number," and that in its enumeration "each shall count as one and only one"; the Aristotelian and post-Kantian, who assert as the end self-realization, understanding by "self" not something particular, but a universal manifested in every man; the evolutionist, who finds the goal to be altruism,—all these, I say, are agreed that all persons have necessarily an equal claim upon the good. The thought of each finds its practical expression in the dictate that we are to strive for a community of the good, for a state of society in which each has an equal share in the ethical, however it may be in the other goods of life.[1]

So if the democratic principle that all men shall share equally in the good life is recognized by all, there is no argument at this point of basic social philosophy. The disagreements commence when men begin to erect theories from this basic position.

If anything is clearly recognized to be a fact, and it is recognized as such by all schools, there is a radical twist in man's intellectual nature, comparable apparently to original sin in his theological make-up, which causes him to ignore that fact, though it be central, or else use it in any way that seems good to him, though the meaning of the fact be the point at issue. Such has been the fate of the fact of the identity of men's interests, of that community in the good which makes the welfare of one the welfare of all.[2]

It is not only that the basic postulate that each individual shall have equal share in the good is accepted by all schools of thought and therefore needs no bolstering; Dewey's confidence on this point, at the time, also stems from his idealistic metaphysics which, as we have seen, originally furnished the foundations for his faith in his ethical postulate. The democratic ideal was now revealed in the historic development of institutions. This position is taken in *The Ethics of Democracy*, written in 1888. He writes here of democracy in such terms as "a manner of life seemingly becoming universal," as "the actual tendencies of political organisms." [3] In this paper, in which he criticizes Sir Henry Maine's book on *Popular Government* from an idealistic, organicist point of view, he says that Maine "sees in democracy no historical meaning, no realization of any ideas." [4] If, for Dewey, Maine would start with a conception of social organism, he would see democracy as the ideal embodied in the existing institutions.

But just as Dewey dropped the metaphysical foundations for his ethical postulate, he turns a few years later to science for support of his democracy. In remarks on the *Future of Science* by Ernest Renan, Dewey in expressing agreement said that what in Hegel had been an attempt at a comprehensive philosophizing of the universe became in Renan the conception and method of the science of philology, a science of the human intellect developing throughout all history. "It is the same law, only considered now as the law of historic growth, not as the dialectic unfolding of the absolute." [5] Instead of the process of dialectic revealing the ideal of democracy, it is science that does so. Science is criticism, analysis.

But science, having carried its analysis, its tearing apart, to the end, finally comes upon the underlying unity; the destruction of the preconceived ideas and institutions only serves to reveal the basic whole. Thus analytic science finally came upon humanity as the unity to which all is to be referred. The work of science is henceforth predominantly synthetic. The unity reveals the law and the end; theory must pass over into practice; knowledge into action. [6]

Thus science not only came upon humanity but is henceforth to become a "social motor."[7] The definition of science "is to know from the standpoint of humanity; its goal is such a sense of life as will enable man to direct his conduct in relation to his fellows by intelligence, not by chance."[8] And the basis of such a scientifically controlled democracy is "a wide distribution of intelligence."[9]

DEMOCRACY AS MEANS

Whether it is science, or the organic view of the dialectic of history, or simply faith based upon a wide and deep interpretation of experience that serves as the foundation for the democratic end, it is an end commonly agreed upon. But there is also the notion of science as a social motor, "universalized in its *range* by coming to include humanity as its subject-matter; universalized in *application* by being made, as to its salient outcome, the common possession of all men."[10] This idea has a close relationship with another side of Dewey's democracy. This is a side which other schools of thought not only ignore, but also one which they never see. That is, a distinctive feature of Dewey's social thought is that democratic ends are inseparable from democratic means. It is not enough for Dewey that each personality shall share in the good; each must also share in the creation of the good. Since the ethical ideal is an ideal for personality, it must be one which the person has power of realizing for himself. He says: "All talk about an ethical ideal is utter nonsense unless man has, or rather is, an end in himself. It is not enough that there be an end which is worked out through man as an instrument; man must himself work out this end."[11]

While *The Ethics of Democracy* may have grounded Dewey's democracy in a metaphysics later discarded, it makes clear the meaning of democracy that abided in his thought. Maine had argued that democracy was only a form of government that had to do with the relation of subject to sovereign and that what differentiated democracy from other forms of government was only a numerical standard; that is, if the sovereign is a multitude and the subject a small number, we have democracy. Dewey objects to the notion that democracy is only a form of government. He says:

A government springs from a vast mass of sentiments, many vague, some defined, of instincts, of aspirations, of hopes and fears, of purposes. It is their reflex and their incorporation; their projection and outgrowth.[12]

Democracy, as well as any other polity, is such an outgrowth, and is thus more than a mere form of government.

Democracy, in a word, is a social, that is to say, an ethical conception, and upon its ethical significance is based its significance as governmental. Democracy is a form of government only because it is a form of moral and spiritual association.[13]

But autocracy is also an ethical conception; and, Dewey says, in the best example of aristocracy known, that of Plato's Republic, the ethical ideal is the development of man's nature so as to bring him into complete harmony with the universe of spiritual relations or, in Platonic language, the state. This, too, is the democratic ideal; so wherein lies the difference? It rests in the means; Plato would have the philosopher-kings set up the conditions for all to share in the good life; but even if this could be accomplished, Dewey would still have a fatal objection. For:

The ethical ideal is not satisfied merely when all men sound the note of harmony with the highest social good, so be it they have not worked it out for themselves. . . . It is true, indeed, that when an individual has found that place in society for which he is best fitted and is exercising the function proper to that place, he has obtained his completed development, but it is also true (and this is the truth omitted by aristocracy, emphasized by democracy) that he must find this place and assume this work in the main for himself.[14]

Democracy, then, is an ethical conception that includes personal responsibility and individual initiative; personality holds the central position; it is the one thing of permanent and abiding worth and lies in each individual.

PRINCIPLES OF DEMOCRACY

From this conception of the worth of unique personalities there results the other principles of democracy: liberty, equality, and fraternity. Democratic liberty does not mean to do as one pleases; freedom is not mere self-assertion or unregulated desire.

Liberty is not a numerical notion of isolation; it is the ethical idea that personality is the supreme and only law, that every man is an absolute end in himself. The democratic ideal includes liberty, because democracy without initiation from within, without an ideal chosen from within and freely followed from within is nothing.[15]

As for equality, it is a mistaken conception that refers to it as a bald numerical individuality where one equals one. Instead, equality refers to the ethical conception of personality:

Personality is as universal as humanity; it is indifferent to all distinctions which divide men from men. Wherever you have a man, there you have a personality, and there is no trace by which one personality may be distinguished from another so as to be set above or below.[16]

Dewey is not content to set forth a theory and leave it to others to make inferences or to devise ways to test it as a guide in action. He expressly states what his conception of equality means in the everyday world of affairs. He notes the claim being made that democracy tends toward socialism, if not toward communism.[17] He admits that "democracy is not in reality what it is in name until it is industrial, as well as civil and political." And the industrial situation is far from this ideal; furthermore, because it is, the result is an imperfect civil and political organization. "For their sakes, therefore, as well as for that of industrial relations, a democracy of wealth is a necessity." [18] But a democracy of wealth is far from implying socialism or communism to the extent that the latter mean a numerical division into equal portions of all wealth, or that somehow society will regulate economic life to the abolition of individual initiative and responsible activity. What democracy of wealth does mean is "that all industrial relations are to be regarded as subordinate to human relations, to the law of personality." [19] Industrial organization must be a social function in the same sense that life in the family is a social function. Dewey asks if individuality is renounced in a family and answers: "I think not; we mean that the family is an ethical community, and that life in the family conforms to its idea only when the individual realizes oneness of interest and purpose with it." [20]

Dewey best explains his meaning of equality by digressing to search for the grounds of objections to the requiredness of a democracy of wealth. The passage that reveals the results of his inquiry is worthy of full quotation:

We still think of life as having two parts, one animal, the other truly human and therefore truly ethical. The getting and distributing of the material benefits of life is regarded as indeed a *means* to the possibility of the higher life, the life of men in their distinctively human relations, but as in themselves wholly outside of that life. Both Plato and Aristotle, for example, always take it as a matter of course, that everything which is industrial, which concerns the getting or distributing of wealth, lies wholly outside, nay, is opposed to the life of the citizen, that is, of the member of an ethical community. Plato's attacks upon the sophists for receiving money for teaching were on the grounds that they thus degraded a personal (that is, a moral) relation, that of teacher and pupil, to an industrial; as if the two were necessarily hostile. Aristotle denies that an artisan can have virtue, i.e., the qualities pertaining to the fulfillment of social functions. Me-

chanics are, indeed, indispensable to the state, "but not all who are indispensable to the state are citizens." (And we must remember that the terms "citizen" and "state" have, in Aristotle, always an ethical bearing.) It was necessary that there should be some who should give themselves to that which is purely material, the industrial, in order that others might have the leisure to give themselves to the social and political, the ethical. We have, nominally, at least, given up the idea that a certain body of men are to be set aside for the doing of this necessary work; but we still think of this work, and of the relations pertaining to it, as if they were outside of the ethical realm and wholly in the natural. We admit, nay, at times we claim, that ethical rules are to be *applied* to this industrial sphere, but we think of it as an external application. That the economic and industrial life is *in itself* ethical, that it is to be made contributory to the realization of personality through the formation of a higher and more complete unity among men, this is what we do not recognize; but such is the meaning of the statement that democracy must become industrial.[21]

Democracy, then, is an ethical conception that includes all of men's experiences, neither only part of each individual's activities, nor but the experiences of a select segment of men. Because of this, moral authority and sovereignty rests in the common will of the people. Dewey pounds this point home in a devasting criticism of Austin's *Jurisprudence* in a paper on "Austin's Theory of Sovereignty," which appeared in 1894.[22] Austin's theory is that law is a command of sovereign to subject, and disobedience of the subject results in punishment from the one issuing the command. Therefore sovereignty must be possessed by a limited and determinate body of persons; thus he identifies sovereignty with government. It is true for Austin that in a sense the opinions and sentiments of the mass of men are supreme. The sovereign habitually defers to them; but such so-called moral law can not be sovereign because sovereignty must be determinate and the opinions and sentiments of men are inchoate, vague, and indeterminate.

Order in a state may rest upon moral law, but it is merely moral and affords no positive direction or command.

Dewey, of course, objects to the notion that sovereignty and government are one; that there is a complete gap between social and moral forces and government itself; that the former cannot state law, while the latter can. His cogent arguments show that Austin's position when logically formulated is untenable. Though Dewey's "wrecking" process is extremely interesting, our purposes are better served by noting the reason for his criticism and the one positive suggestion he finds in Austin. Dewey says:

At all events, I would raise the question whether there is any alternative between a theory like Austin's, which, placing sovereignty in a part of society, makes government an entity *per se*, whose operations are all commands, and a theory which finds the residence of sovereignty in the whole complex of social activities, thus making a government an organ—an organ the more efficient, we may add, just in proportion as it is not an entity *per se*, but is flexible and responsible to the social whole, or true sovereign.[23]

Dewey believes that those who accept the first position, and thus reject Rousseau's idea of sovereignty as resident in the common will, must, if they are logical, fall into all the difficulties of Austin's position. However, Dewey seizes upon Austin's notion of determinateness and gives it a definite place in his own position. For he recognizes that sovereignty must be determinate in order to avoid vagueness, chaos, or anarchy. So, while he accepts Rousseau's common will, it needs the determinateness sought by Austin. Dewey says:

The great weakness of Rousseau's theory that the general will is sovereign, is that he makes its generality exclude all special modes of operation. While, then, Austin's identification of the determinate factor with a specified group of individuals seems indefensible, yet in insisting that sovereignty requires determinate forms of exercise he is guarding us against the error which would make generality equivalent to vagueness.[24]

Sovereignty, then, inheres in the masses; for order, force, effectiveness of sovereignty, there must be specific modes of operation; democracy needs most of all method of expressing its determinateness, its common will. The foremost problem that must be solved within a democratic society is the problem of method, method which will locate and express the common will.

In summary, Dewey's democracy means that each unique personality is of incomparable worth and shall share equally in the good; he shall share, not only in the good as an end, but also in the means of creating the good. All of his experiences are included with those of all his fellows as having an ethical bearing. The sovereignty implicit in this community of ethical experience needs methods of specific operation for its expression. The social motor that can provide this direction is science, science that means to know from the standpoint of humanity.

PROXIMATE GOALS

The criticism may be voiced that Dewey's conception of the good life as that attained in the process of its creation by community effort and his emphasis on method give no goal toward which men may strive.[25] Merle Curti, in his account of Dewey's social ideas, points out the latter's use of proximate goals. He says:

Any discussion of Dewey's social objectives must be both prefaced by and penetrated with his unqualified repudiation of fixed goals. Yet in spite of his adherence to the idea of an open universe in which change and growth are the paramount characteristics, Dewey, in the concrete and realistic spirit of instrumentalism, has concerned himself with approximate goals or next steps. These proximate goals may be best understood by the specific criticisms which he has made of actualities in the world about him.[26]

A few of Dewey's specific criticisms of the existing situation should demonstrate his concrete suggestions for the next steps needed to implement democracy. We have just had occasion to note his charge that there was an aristocracy of industrial relations and that the fuller and freer development of the democratic ideal would be held in check until there was a democracy of wealth, until economic relations were subordinated to human relations. We have also seen that Dewey was opposed to the principle of charity; he took the position that the goal should be to remove the conditions in society that made charity a necessity. He points to social conditions as breeding poverty in a paper on "Galton's Statistical Methods." He says:

The tendency of wealth to breed wealth, as illustrated by any interest table, and the tendency of extreme poverty to induce conditions which plunge children still deeper into poverty would probably prevent the operation of the law of regression toward mediocrity.[27]

He adds that something like a normal curve might result if there grew up new industrial relations which would lessen the value of old forms of wealth, or if there were a development of social relations which would increase the ambition and chances of the poor.

Dewey later suggests that the industrial problem is an ethical problem of the most serious kind because under the existing economic relations the worker does not appreciate the significance or bearing of what he does; "and he does not perform his work because of sharing in a larger scientific and social consciousness. If he did, he would be free. All other proper accompaniments of wages and hours, healthful and inspiring conditions would be added unto him, because he would have entered into the ethical kingdom." [28] Not only are the "proper accompaniments" and "inspiring conditions" lacking for adult workers but also for children. He says in

"Evolutionary Method as Applied to Morality" that "what our
moral code permits is, to condemn hundreds and thousands of
little children, as well as grown people, to sickly, stunted, and
defective lives, physical as well as mental." [29] He adds that it
is true that many persons attack this state of affairs as immoral,
but, lacking a democratic point of view, they feel that such
conditions are necessary and an inevitable incident in the
whole industrial order and cannot be changed without shaking
society.

These statements should suffice to show that Dewey has no
difficulty locating positive proximate goals for the democratic
process. The same perspective that points to these concrete
ends provides the standpoint from which he views the general
trends of the present society in which the school must function.
This outline sketch of present social conditions is described
in *School and Society*.[30] That it is only a sketch is because
the changing social conditions "are writ so large that he who
runs may read." [31]

What Dewey sees in the changes of the past century is the
most rapid and complete revolution in history. It is foremost an
industrial revolution brought about by science and technology;
the growth of invention resulted in a world-wide market as
the object of production, with vast centers of population and
cheap and rapid means of communication and transportation
to supply this market. Through the revolution,

The face of the earth is making over, even as to its physical forms;
political boundaries are wiped out and moved about as if they were
indeed only lines on a paper map; population is hurriedly gathered from the ends of the earth; habits of living are altered with
startling abruptness and thoroughness; the search for the truths
of nature is infinitely stimulated and facilitated and their application to life made not only applicable, but commercially necessary.
Even our moral and religious ideas and interests, the most conservative because the deepest-lying things in our nature, are pro-
foundly affected.[32]

At the beginning of the revolutionary period there was the neighborhood system where the household was the center around which all the typical forms of industrial occupations were carried on and the entire productive process stood revealed. For all the family, including the children, there was immediate personal concern and involvement and actual participation in the industrial processes at an early age. Dewey felt that there was great value for discipline and character building in this system. It provided:

Training in the habits of order and industry, and in the idea of responsibility, of obligation to do something, to produce something in the world. . . . there was continual training of observation, of ingenuity, constructive imagination, of logical thought, and of the sense of reality acquired through firsthand contact with actualities.[33]

At the time of Dewey's social analysis, however, all this had changed; these values no longer accrued to household and neighborhood occupations. The revolution, with its concentration of industry and its division of labor, had practically eliminated or isolated the household occupations from the continuous and complete processes of social production. Yet the new industrial system had brought with it some advantages and compensations. These Dewey describes as

The increase in toleration, in breadth of social judgment, the larger acquaintance with human nature, the sharpened alertness in reading signs of character and interpreting social situations, greater accuracy of adaptation to differing personalities, contact with greater commercial activities.[34]

So Dewey did not suffer from nostalgia and desire to return to the past, for the past life was narrow and restricting, of too great immediate concern for mere existence. The newer life gave promise of much fuller and freer experiences. The problem of society, as Dewey saw it, was how to retain the advantages made possible by the revolution and yet safeguard and

restore the values of old. This was the problem of the society in which the school operated and was thus the problem of the school.

SOME IMPLICATIONS FOR EDUCATION

Any one-sided conception of democracy that views its principles as only relating to ends and not means seems unable to escape ultimately an aristocratic position. Hence educational practices based upon such a conception would probably retain the old aristocratic divisions between the spiritual and the mundane, the animal and the human, between desire and will, and the material and ethical. Education so based would likely ignore the everyday problems of men, seek to control and restrict animal desire, and might choose between those pupils who must attend to the material and those who may enter fully the ethical kingdom. So-called democratic ends without democratic method for the formation of those ends would apparently lead to authoritarian selection of the proximate goals and result in indoctrination of passive individuals who must accept their station in relation to those ends, who must adjust themselves to preconceived conditions, and, where they fail, must submit to a pathological education.

This seems to mean that the curriculum of the school might either be directed to the "finer" and "higher" things of life to the exclusion of the practical needs of men and of society, or that there might be two curricula, one for the necessary workers who provide the means for the higher life, and one for those who enter upon the latter. Method would probably be an individual, competitive process to determine those fitted for the separate stations. It would seem ultimately to be pathological method in the sense that each individual must be coerced, exhorted, drilled, cajoled, and inhibited toward his proper place so that society will not be disrupted.

On the other hand, Dewey's more complete view of democracy makes three primary demands upon the school. In the first place, Dewey's requirement for democracy includes the principle that common goals be formulated and worked out by common means. The method of locating the goals and planning their realization must be a community method. No school organized on an individualistic, competetive basis can ever effect this principle in practice. So the school must be organized as a community where children are provided the opportunity and the direction for experimentation in methods of decision, planning, and cooperative effort that will best allow them to build and realize their aims. We saw that democratic sovereignty needs methods of expressing its determinateness. The school, not only as a democratic community itself, but for the larger community which it serves, must train pupils in methods of locating and expressing their common will.

But the development and statement of a community of will is not something in itself, something that takes place in isolation; it grows out of the concrete activities of individuals and involves the relationships of these activities to the interests and problems of the society as a whole. Since these concerns center about men's occupations, the latter must be the content of education in the school. As children in the school engage in the dominant occupations, as they study the relationships among occupations and the connections of the work of the everyday world with art, science, religion, they are in the same setting out of which common moral values developed in the history of the race. Whereas the latter grew up with inadequate methods and with too immediate concern for economic return, the school is free from this necessity and can concentrate upon the improvement of modes of operation that will enhance the building of moral values.

The second demand made by Dewey's conception of democracy is that the ethical world must include all of the experiences of men. In Dewey's opinion, ever since the time of

the Greeks, men's industrial activities have been excluded from this sphere. Not, of course, as he says, that moral principles were never to be applied to our economic system, but in the sense that the work of the mechanic, the artisan, did not in itself have ethical quality. The moral element resided in every occupation whether theory conceived it so or not; and while life was simple, as long as it provided close contact with the actualities of nature and social development, men, perhaps unconsciously, saw this moral element in its bearings in the life of society. But the industrial revolution had eliminated this close relationship with simple realities; men no longer could see the larger meaning involved in their occupations; their lives were being divided, one part being given over to work, the other to living. To the extent that Aristotle's division did not prevail for segments of men, it existed now within men. The requirement for education was to overcome this division, to extend the ethical kingdom. Since the problem of the new industrial society was how to make it possible for men to regain their bearings, to enable them to see the meaning and significance of their daily work in relation to their whole natural and social environment, these daily occupations and these same relationships must become the content provided by the school.

The method of the school must be active participation in the most typical occupations, partly, perhaps, to overcome class bias, the feeling of distinctiveness and superiority of intellectual work as against work with the hands. But, more important, it is when individuals attempt to do something, to realize their ideas, that social relationships become involved, and this means that moral qualities pervade the act; action, conduct, includes the ethical. Therefore ethical training comes in the process of endeavoring to reach objectives, not in passive, individualistic absorption or adjustment to an external ethical code.

The third requirement that results from Dewey's conception of democracy is again an extension of the ethical world in the

sense that it is to include not only all the experiences of men
but the experiences of all men. By men is meant all individuals; there must be no division between the child and adult
worlds, where the latter is ethical and the former mere preparation, or test by ordeal, to qualify for entrance upon the
ethical life.[35] Therefore the life and experiences of the children
in the school must be continuous with the activities of the
outside, adult world. The point of closest contact of children
with adult institutions is in the area of occupations, not with
the refinements and abstract products of art, religion, and
science. Just as men's more removed interest in art, religion,
and music developed in their relationship with their immediate interests and activities—their occupations—so will the
interest of children similarly develop.

Dewey believed that in the preindustrial society the gap
between child and adult was easily bridged by the early sharing
of the child in the household and neighborhood occupations,
which provided training in the habits and values of the adult
world and insight into their relationships to the actualities of
life. This bridge, weakened by the industrial revolution, and
further shaken by forcing the child into another, and separated
and isolated, life of the formal school, must be strengthened
and restored by doing away with this other distinct life, and
supplanting it with a school life that will provide the opportunity for discipline and responsibility formerly supplied by the
household and neighborhood occupations. If the content and
method of the school centers in these occupations, the division
between school and life, between child and adult worlds, can be
removed and continuity achieved. Furthermore, other problems created by the revolution, the loss of significance of work
caused by the division of labor, the loss of firsthand contact
with the natural world, and the loss of bearing due to the
bewildering advance and spread of new knowledge caused by
science and developments in communication facilities—all such
losses can be redeemed if the meaning of our new work and

new knowledge is related to the dominant occupations that make it possible for men to be at home in the physical world.

Dewey's democracy points definitely to the social organization of the school with occupations as the central content and method. But Dewey was not alone in recognizing some of the difficulties confronting education. Others saw some of the same difficulties and developed theories and prescribed practices to meet them. While they did not see all the problems in the same, or in as wide, context as Dewey, nevertheless he was aware of their suggestions and these undoubtedly had a bearing on the policies and practices of his experimental school. It is, therefore, some of these major movements and Dewey's reactions to them that are examined in the next chapter.

· VI ·

DEWEY'S REACTIONS TO OTHER EDUCATIONAL MOVEMENTS OF THE TIME

IT MAY SEEM TRITE to state that John Dewey was not the only educational thinker of the period under consideration. What, perhaps, is less obvious and well known is that the development of Dewey's thought which culminated in his experimental school took form in a time of unusual vigor, novelty, and enthusiasm in educational speculation and programmatic change. Whether Dewey was distinctive among all the active educators of his day because of his method of careful scrutiny of the foundational disciplines, in addition to strictly educational studies, need not here be debated. But the wide scope of his interests and thinking did include careful and critical study of the current ideas and the works of his colleagues among the professional educators. In fact, he actively participated by membership in organizations and through the medium of his critical writings in the newer educational movements instigated by others.

It is clear, then, that any effort to assess the thinking that lay behind his experimental school must include a study of his reactions to the distinct educational movements of the day. Explicitly formulated in his papers are his interpretations and criticisms of four vital tendencies in the current educational scene: (1) The Herbartian Movement; (2) The Child Study Movement; (3) The Manual Training Movement; and (4) W. T. Harris and Traditional Education.[1]

THE HERBARTIAN MOVEMENT

The Herbartian Theory

The first and second yearbooks (1895 and 1896) of the newly formed Herbart Society for the Scientific Study of Teaching, of whose executive council Dewey was a member, were devoted to the problem of the selection, sequence, and articulation of the studies of the curriculum. Charles DeGarmo gave the setting for the problem.[2] In his view, the preceding forty or fifty years of American education had been occupied with the effort to extend the benefits of education to all the people; the urgent problem had been the establishment of facilities and machinery for the successful prosecution of this expanding educational enterprise. Beginning when there were few things to learn—language, logic, and philosophy—and few persons to learn them—gentlemen, clergymen, and professionals—this development, as DeGarmo saw it in 1895, now faced two difficulties: the vast increase in available knowledge and the multiplication of learners. Since the former subjects of study were of little use to the "sons of toil," and since there were many new areas of subject-matter from which to choose, educators were forced to consider the problem of what to teach.

Before determining what to teach, however, the purpose of instruction must be made clear. Again, there had been a change from the earlier conceptions which expected intellectual training from the State with ethical training reserved for the Church. But DeGarmo, following Herbart, was prepared to restrict the Church to the teaching of theological dogma and ecclesiastical ceremony and to accept the public school as an adequate agency for the development of moral character. If character training supplants mere mental training as the purpose of public education, then the emphasis in the curriculum must shift from formal disciplines to the content studies that give insight into fundamental ethical ideals.

The end—moral character—being established, the Herbartians chose the child's apperception as their guide in the selection of the content of education. Just what apperception means and how it serves as a guide when combined with the theory of culture epochs is concisely described by Frank M. McMurry:

The principle of apperception declares that what one can know and feel and will depends on what he has already known and felt and willed, or that past experiences are the sole basis for intellectual, emotional, and ethical growth. Accordingly, excellence in teaching consists, first of all, in fitting newly offered ideas closely to these past experiences as their base or foundation. The first requisite to this end is that the subject-matter of instruction be intimately related both to the kind of thinking and to the topics of thought which most naturally occupy the child's mind. Suitable matter will vary according to age and stage of development. There is probably a period in each person's life when any book, or indeed any thought, can be most highly appreciated. If we could only discover and take advantage of this most opportune moment for offering every bit of knowledge, what a wonderful economy of effort would result! Children's brains would then continually be stirred by what they received at school. The theory of the culture epochs, i.e., that the child passes through the same general stages of development through which the race passes, is influencing teachers to select courses of study with special reference to the fitness of their subject-matter for certain stages of child-growth. If the development of the race is in general like that of the child, what specially interested the former at a certain age will appeal with most force to the latter at the corresponding age; consequently that is what should be given to him. By this arrangement the content of each study can be fitted more closely to the child's past experiences and become more fully a part of him. That means that a high degree of apperception will be secured; the theory of the culture epochs is, therefore, only a subdivision of the very broad principle of apperception.[3]

Therefore, for the Herbartians, the mind, the emotions, the will—that is, the total character—are built by the proper presentation of ideas. Two traditional methods of selecting and presenting the right ideas must be abandoned: one, the relative ease of acquisition or the relative simplicity, and two, the logical order in the subject-matter. The substitute demanded is the principle of the culture epochs, where the task is to find the parallelism between the "stage" of the child and the corresponding "epoch" in the race.

There is another important subdivision of apperception in addition to the principle of the culture epochs for the selection of ideas—the principle of concentration.[4] There is the danger that even with the presentation of the right ideas at the right time there may result distinct and unrelated spheres of thought, something similar to the situation in which a pupil does not associate the "Spain" and the "Genoa" of the Columbus story with the "Spain" and the "Genoa" of the geography lesson. The need, then, is for concentration, for a core study with which all parts of the course of study must be associated. McMurry states that "recent pedagogy declares that the *number* and *closeness* of relations into which an idea enters are as important as the vividness and accuracy with which it is conceived; hence the relationship among facts is becoming a separate and great topic in school work, and in all teaching."[5] There was considerable agreement that some technique of association was neccessary; there was common opinion that content as opposed to form material should be the core; but what that content should be proved to be a problem eliciting much stubborn controversy. The block resided in the question of the ethical worth of the subject-matter.

It must be remembered that the end of education was moral, the development of character; it was not simply the building of closely related ideas into an apperceptive mass. There were those who held that history and literature, the former for upper grades, the latter for beginning grades, should be given the most prominent position in the course of study. Others said nature study, by which they meant science, should be the core; some narrowed nature study to geography. The first group argued that history and literature "not only impart a knowledge of what is right and wrong." [6] On the other hand nature study was defended because it would put a child in sympathy with nature. "It should be to his heart what winter is to the apple, a mellowing, softening influence." [7] So went the debate, with all agreeing, however, on the prime necessity of a content that was most conducive to moral training.

The majority, perhaps, favored history and literature as the subjects of concentration. But there was one strongly dissenting voice, that of Mr. Galbreath, who asked: "May not a boy learn the economic relations of mankind––how science is exchanged for service––and come to himself ethically through a study of geography? Will not insight into scientific principles and a knowledge of their application to the arts and industries in his environment affect his 'ethical standpoint'? Will not the skill and conscious power acquired through manual training tend to augment the number of high and firm resolutions?" [8] After posing these question Mr. Galbreath suggested that concentration "must include the relation that naturally exists between an idea and the corresponding effort that tends to realize it." [9]

Dewey's Interpretation and Criticism

Galbreath's comments serve to introduce Dewey's response to the theory of apperception and its subdivisions, culture epochs and concentration. For in his "Interpretation of the Culture-Epoch Theory," Dewey approves these remarks by Galbreath and says that their bearing is wide.[10] After crediting Mr. Galbreath, he goes on to state his own interpretation. He admits that he does not question the correspondence between culture epochs and the stages of individual development in a "general way." But he insists that the upholders of

the theory take cultural *products* as the object of study; it apparently never occurred to them, he thinks, to question this point and possibly arrive with him to the point of considering the correspondence between the child's interest and the psychical conditions which originated these products.[11] For Dewey, the correspondence is between the life and interest of the epoch and the life and interest of the child. What is the life and interest of the child?

Children are interested directly in present life, in the social conditions which exist all about them and with which they come in contact; and any genuine, and educative historic interest is simply a reflex of this interest in the *existing* social structure.[12]

Character development for Dewey, then, comes not through presentation of ideas at the right time and in the right relationships—ideas that were the results of the life and struggle of others—but through the effort to realize ideas developing from the present impulses of the child amidst his surroundings. Obviously, history and literature cannot be the subjects of concentration; the curriculum must center about problems of living in today's world. Does this mean that there is no place for history, for the great epochs of past culture? In the light of Dewey's interest in evolution, in genesis and development, this would hardly be consistent. Certainly the study of the great ages of history is important, provided the proper interpretation is made.

Perhaps the contrast between Dewey's view and that of the Herbartians can be more clearly indicated by a brief look at their respective treatment of the myth. For the Herbartians, there was an epoch when men were inspired to wild and fantastic imaginations that resulted in the products of fancy we call myths. Children too pass through a stage of naive and flighty comparisons of widely different experiences. When children are in this stage the time is ripe for them to be presented with the myths of the race. There are two purposes to be served. First, the Herbartians believed that the material must interest the child; the child "naturally" will be interested in myths when in the "fantastic imagination" stage. Secondly, it is a stage a child *must* go through before he reaches the stage where he can appreciate the higher ethical products of later epochs in the history of the race.

For Dewey, on the other hand, "the myth is a complete social product, reflecting in itself the intellectual, the economic, and the political condition of a certain people." He would admit myths to his course of study, not because they were interesting, not because they were—though of no immediate value—necessary for later development, but because a myth had value to a child if he "has been led for himself first to appreciate the natural facts and the social conditions which are reflected in it." [13] True, it is today's intellectual, economic, and political conditions that he says children are interested in and it is their efforts to realize their ideas in existing conditions that form their characters. Yet a study of myths can be a means to this end in two ways. First, in leading a child to "appreciate the natural facts and social conditions" in the relatively simple societies that produced the myths, he will more readily see similar relationships in his own more complex society. Secondly, these myths may still be a part of modern mind even though they may have no relationship to existing conditions— the knowledge of which fact would be of no little influence in the development of the child's character.

While Dewey's specific interpretation of myths and their use in education may not be of general interest, it points toward his notion of the error in the usual correspondence theory of culture epochs. He states concisely what the mistake is in his "Interpretation of Savage Mind," which appeared in 1902:

The psychical attitudes and traits of the savage are more than stages through which mind has passed, leaving them behind. They are outgrowths which have entered decisively into further

evolution, and as such form an integral part of the framework of present mental organization.[14]

It is fallacious, then, to study the culture epochs in terms of present civilized mind as the standard against which earlier stages are inferior. Such a method yields only a haphazard, uncontrollable collection of static facts. If apperception is to be the guide for the selection of materials of instruction, if number and closeness of relations into which an idea enters is the great topic in school work as the Herbartians claim, then we should study the epochs for some coherent scheme of mind, for a pattern in its constituent elements.

If we look for the pattern with an awareness that the mind is an instrument for controlling the environment in relation to the ends of the life process, we find in any social group similar special functions to which mind is relative. These special functions are the occupations, Dewey discloses:

Occupations determine the fundamental modes of activity, and hence control the formation and use of habits. These habits, in turn, are something more than practical and overt. "Apperceptive masses" and associational tracts of necessity conform to the dominant activities. The occupations determine the chief modes of satisfaction, the standards of success and failure. Hence they furnish the working classifications and definitions of value; they control the desire processes. Moreover, they decide the sets of objects and relations that are important, and thereby provide the content or material of attention, and the qualities that are interestingly significant. The direction given to mental life thereby extends to emotional and intellectual characteristics. So fundamental and pervasive is the group of occupational activities that it affords the scheme or pattern of the structural organization of mental traits. Occupations integrate special elements into a functional whole.[15]

In any society then, including the present, the group of occupations is the dominant activity to which both interest and value accrue. These were the two elements that the Herbar-

tians sought in study *about* the cultural products of history.
If the proper selection from among these products were made
and presented to children, ethical characters could be developed. But for Dewey, as for Galbreath, ethical character
developed through the process of realization of the child's own
ideas and interests. Since the child was interested in the social
activities about him and since the occupations of mankind are
the integrating force of these activities, both the method and
content of instruction should be these occupations.

It should be emphasized here that this is no narrowly conceived physical activity that stops short of guidance toward the
intellectual, scientific, aesthetic, and ethical aspirations and
achievements of humanity. At the conclusion of his paper on
"Interpretation of Savage Mind," Dewey reminds us that "the
adjustment of habits to ends, through the medium of a problematic, doubtful, precarious situation, is the structual form
upon which present intelligence and emotion are built." [16]
The common precarious situations in life involve basically
men's ways of making a living. But between the active impulse that meets with this problem and its consummatory close
there is the social process of mediation that develops all the
division of labor, objective instrumentalities and contents, the
intellectual tools, emotional commitments, and spiritual ideals
of men. To achieve the integrated ethical character sought by
the Herbartians through "concentration," Dewey would have
children engage in the social process by which these mediating
agencies developed about the core of dominant activities of the
race—the occupations. Thus children would come to know and
understand the logically organized disciplines in their relations with the realities from which they sprang, and hence he
would avoid the gravest obstacle to the development of ethical
character—the separation of these disciplines from the existential conditions which give them their reason for being.

THE CHILD STUDY MOVEMENT

The Movement

The widespread interest in child study was, in Illinois, closely allied with the Herbartian movement. The Illinois Society for Child-Study, organized in 1895, claimed many of the Herbartians as members and gained Dewey's attention and participation as a member of its Advisory Board and Executive Committee. In the report of the transactions of this society, C. C. Van Liew traces the evolution of the movement:

The idea of child-study may be distinctly seen in Comenius's plea for objective instruction and the training of the senses; in Rousseau's extreme principle of a return to nature and the precedence of physical education; in Pestalozzi's untiring labors in behalf of the rights of sense-perception; in Froebel's emphasis of motor activity and the play impulse in the child's growth; and finally in Herbart's system of education as based upon the psychological and ethical nature of man.[17]

It was this background of thought that led to the notion that not life-ideals, nor specific ends, nor mere traditional usages should determine the construction of educational systems but that the claims of the educable being himself should be the significant guiding factor.

What these claims were varied with the individual, but they could now be discovered by science. Science meant, in this movement, observation of individuals and painstaking record keeping with the consequent massing of data that could be sifted and analyzed in a search for law. Enthusiastic observers reported thousands of such records detailed as to every movement of the child and often embellished with partial and sentimental interpretations. One principle, thus determined, that changed educational practice was the law of physical development from the mass activity of the large muscles to the more intricate and specific functions of the small muscles. This law tended to reverse the Froebelian "occupations" of the kindergarten from close manipulation of small objects, such as in the popular needlework, toward activities initially engaging a large part, or all, of the body; it was such a concept, for example, that introduced the Palmer Method in writing. Another result of the close observation of children was the disclosure that physical defects, of hearing, of sight, and of other bodily functions, were the cause of the difficulties many ch ldren experienced in their schoolwork. Probably this finding led to the most permanent outcome of the whole child study movement, namely, the more humane and considerate treatment of each individual child.

Dewey's Interpretation and Criticism

In spite of some accomplishments, the child study movement was soon assailed by many critics, among whom was Dewey. In attempting to explain the source of the criticisms, he said:

The feature of child-study against which criticism has been justly directed are the results partly of the exaggerations incident to all large movements in their inception, partly of the misdirected gyrations of those camp-followers who, hanging about education as about all other progressive forces, attempt to use child study for their own advertising and aggrandizement, and partly of the unwise zeal of those who, lacking in stability, are blown about by every new wind of doctrine and lose the just perspective.[18]

It is probable that this harsh assessment of the cause of the movement's difficulties stems from what must have been his disgust for the reams of gushing, sentimental, and almost mystical idealizations of any and every bit of expressiveness on the part of children.

More pertinent for our purpose, however, is his own criticism, made by quoting William James to the effect that "the

mere collection of facts, uncontrolled by working hypotheses, unenlightened by generalization, never made a science and never will." [19] For Dewey the method of child study was quackery and the results confusion unless it could be taken out of its isolation and placed into its true relationship with the genetic development of education in the struggles of the race.

This relationship Dewey attempts to locate in his paper "The Interpretation Side of Child-Study." [20] He seeks to answer the question "What is the source of this interest in child life?" He finds three sources in three great movements in the history of the race and he terms them the political, the aesthetic, and the scientific. Admitting that there is always interest in and concern for the child, nevertheless, he maintains that there are three periods in Western history when this interest and concern was *consciously* directed toward child study and they came at times of greatest conflict in society. He says:

All these three interests of which I shall speak this evening, the practical or political, the aesthetic, and the scientific, came at times of great agitations of life—at times when old institutions were being transformed, when there was a conflict between civilizations and races previously separated, when life was in a ferment, and when it was necessary for persons to reflect upon the meaning of life and to attempt to settle for themselves some well-defined and established principles which would afford a basis for holding life together, for organizing it. [21]

The first such period was in the time of Plato and Aristotle. Their society was breaking down and they looked consciously at the child as an instrument for the achievement of stable political organization. Thus, routine and tradition could not serve to educate the child; he must be trained systematically to take his place in the ideal social structure in view. Dewey says:

The interest in education and in the child originated, then, because man recognized that social life was capable of intelligent direction. The first step at getting at this direction was to begin with the child and prepare him from the first for the type of social life held in view. As this was the first, so it is today still the deepest and best organized motive in popular consciousness both for education and for attention to the child.[22]

Important as this source of interest in the child was, it was incomplete and dangerous; it was incomplete because the child was not taken in himself, was not observed as he is, and only those facts of child life could be seen which were related to the end in view; it was dangerous because it tended to rigidity, mechanism, and arbitrary schemes of imposition.

The second period of crisis was the time of the Renaissance and this led to what Dewey termed the aesthetic interest in the child. The conflict between medieval Christianity and Hellenic learning created a conscious interest in the child as a symbol, retrospective as a sign of man's lost innocence, lost promise, and prospective as a hope of what humanity might become. Dewey says:

I take it that the child was recognized now as having this prophetic value; the child life was recognized as somehow pointing forward not simply to some particular form of social life, but rather as a dream of some social life which as yet they could not formulate, which lay either too far beyond or too far behind.[23]

Now this aesthetic interest in the child is an advance over the purely political interest. Rather than fitting the child into a fixed social order, the child becomes a clue to what that social order should be. Yet the gulf between the real, actual limitations of life and the ideal set up remained so that the aesthetic interest tended to become merely sentimental and romantic. So in spite of the fact that this interest motivated art in all its forms and did help humanity find its ideal, it too was incomplete.

Gradually the evil tendencies of the interest which has its source in the aesthetic point of view, tends to reinforce, or rather correct,

the other; each emphasizes and sets the other off. The school only too often stands for the mechanical routine side, while the home stands for the child as a plaything, a symbol, something to make life more agreeable, more happy for the adult.[24]

The third great movement is that of modern times when old habits and traditions—physical, national, social, industrial, moral, and religious—are breaking down. The scientific interest that helped to bring about the crisis led to conscious interest in the child as one feature in the interest in growth and evolution on which modern science focused. There is a tendency in this scientific interest in the child to study him as a mere object of curiosity; at best this adds a third interest; at worst, it supersedes the political and aesthetic interests. For Dewey, both the latter purposes must be retained and the scientific interest used to reinforce, correct, and vivify them. He says:

For the practical interest, as we have said of the aesthetic, the scientific type is not a substitute; neither, again, is it superimposed upon the other two. It is these other interests which set the problem, which furnish the end, which make the demand for science, and it is science and science alone which can respond to these demands and can solve the problems which the emotional idealistic interest and the practical or political interest made.[25]

In these passages Dewey makes it clear that he sees the current social scene as one of rapid change, when old institutions are being transformed and it becomes increasingly difficult to meet the political interest in a well-organized society and equally hard to satisfy the conditions for the development of the aesthetic interest in the individual as a human personality. Difficult as the situation is, there is a new interest in the child that holds promise of fruitful attack on the problem —the scientific interest. But this interest must be properly focused; three possible foci for science must be avoided. First, scientific study of the child must *not* be for objective curiosity —for the sake of science itself. Second, it must *not* be a mere search of child life for the psychological principles of growth as exhibited by their present behavior. Third, it must *not* seek the individual adjustments necessary to maintain current society in an orderly fashion, nor the methods of manipulation of the child for such adjustments. Instead of any of these isolated approaches, science must seek to encompass the wider problem of the relation of the individual's self-realization to the social organization and welfare. Not until the conscious interest in the child concentrates upon him as a center of creativeness within a common social, political structure, and thus spans the gulf separating the individual from society, will scientific child study yield the results necessary to deal with the current agitations of a rapidly changing world.

THE MANUAL TRAINING MOVEMENT

Background

In 1880, Dr. Calvin M. Woodward opened his St. Louis Manual Training School. This event gave impetus to what is known as the Manual Training Movement, a distinct and vigorous trend in education during the following two decades. For many years prior to this period there had been an exchange of what Arthur B. Mays terms confused and ill-defined ideas of vocational, industrial, or technical education.[26] There were many shades of opinion supporting two basic points of view. On one hand, a minority demanded, for a variety of reasons, that some sort of training for a life of work be given a place in the public schools. On the other hand, a majority maintained that the purpose of the public, or common, schools was to train students for, as they put it, the work of life. That is, for this group the school's function was to raise the general level of "culture." Training for a job was an individual or family matter or a concern of industry, that growing institution which was demanding better trained workers.

It seems plausible that another source of the confusion over this issue can be traced to the growing opposition to the traditional "bookish" education. The movement away from the conception of the learner as one engaged in passive absorption, and toward the notion of his active appropriation of knowledge, had begun. The self-activity of the Froebelian "occupations" had flourished in the kindergartens. No doubt many an educator, unhappy with traditional programs, somewhat encouraged by the activity movement, yet still clinging to the concept of culture as refined and labor as crude and menial, was torn by inner conflict which often made his position in regard to vocational education confused, if not absurd.

It was in such a setting that the Manual Training Movement appeared—and made headway, it may be ventured, because of these conflicts. For the slogan of its founder, Woodward, was to "put the whole boy to school, his hands as well as his head." His notion was that manual work was to discipline the "mechanical faculties" as the classics might discipline the "mental." Woodward's scheme is more fully stated by his colleague, President Runkle of the Massachusetts Institute of Technology. The latter is quoted by Mays:

We abstract all the mechanical processes and manual arts and typical tools of the trades and occupations of men, arrange a systematic course of instruction in the same, and then incorporate it into our system of education. Thus without teaching any trade we teach the essential mechanical principles of all.[27]

Even the culturalist might make himself believe that such manual discipline helped train for the "work of life." At the same time, a by-product might be some training for the life of work—enough to satisfy temporarily the less extreme of the vocationalists. While such a compromise might afford a rallying ground, as is usual with such partial solutions, dissension was soon renewed. In spite of the claims of universal abstraction from all the trades and occupations, cooking, carpentry, and sewing were the manual arts actually included to any important extent. It soon became clear that this was an unsatisfactorily narrow program for the vocationalists, and the culturalists still unconsciously cringed at the sound of saws in the sacred halls of learning.

At the close of the century there were sharply divergent views. These are concisely summed up by Mays:

On the whole, the thinking of most leaders during the closing years of the nineteenth century betrayed a fear that the traditional cultural forms of school education would be displaced by some sort of vocational education which would be wholly utilitarian and the "higher faculties of the mind" would be utterly neglected. Some welcomed the nonvocational manual training as a happy compromise with the forces of the social and economic environment which were demanding a change in the curriculum. Others seemed to feel that an uncompromising defense of the traditional curriculum was the only hope for the future of general education. Still others were receptive to the idea of the introduction of courses into the public schools which would contribute directly to vocational competency.[28]

Dewey's Interpretation and Criticism

Such was the thinking at the close of the nineteenth century; this coincides with the period of operation of the Dewey School. No doubt, it is on the basis of his knowledge of this thought and of his evidence from his own experimental school that Dewey offers his own judgment in 1903. He said then:

We are emerging from a time in which manual training and constructive work are regarded, in the lower grades, as a form of "busy-work" or a concession to the desire of the child for amusement, and in the upper grades as having a distinctively technical, or even utilitarian and professional aim.[29]

This statement suggests that with his customary approach Dewey has reconstructed the problem from the either-or

variety of activity vs. passivity and culture vs. vocation. We find such a reformulation of the problem in this statement:

First, what group of studies will most serviceably recognize the typical divisions of labor, the typical callings in society, callings which are absolutely indispensable to the spiritual as well as to the material ends of society; and secondly, not to do detriment to the real culture of the individual, or, if this seems too negative a statement, to secure for him the full use and control of his own powers.[30]

It is clear that Dewey refuses to support a distinctively utilitarian view of the place of vocational training; yet it is equally obvious that he does not share the culturalist's fears of the effect of adding meanly practical studies to the school program. In fact, for him, there is nothing in any study or calling itself that makes it low or menial; it only seems so, merely because it has been condemned to isolation from the ethical world. Furthermore, Dewey makes it plain that he is not interested in vocational work for the mere satisfaction of the principle of activity, or as he calls it, "busy-work." Vocational studies must first serve the ethical ends of society and, secondly, they must expand and relate the growing experiences of the individual. Vocations represent the serious and permanent interests of humanity; they furnish the basic reason and the sphere of application for the so-called higher or scholastic studies, and so must be included in the program of the school. Dewey says, "To ignore them, to deny them a rightful position in the educational circle, is to maintain within society that very cleft between so-called material and spiritual interests which it is the business of education to strive to overcome."[31] Vocational study should be included not only to bridge this gap between the material and the spiritual but also to span the tremendous distance between child and adult worlds. For, Dewey says:

The newcomers into civilization find themselves face to face with technical, mechanical, the intellectual devices and resources in the development of which they have had no share or lot; and which are so far beyond them that they have no instinctive or natural means of understanding them. The problem of education—the problem of establishing vital connections between the immature child and the cultural and technical achievements of adult life—thus continually increases in difficulty.[32]

There is in Dewey's thinking, then, ideas which support the culturalist's contention that public education is to prepare for the work of life—but with a vital difference. For he would include, as an integral part of the work of life, a life of work in one of the occupations of humanity. In the early years of schooling, the typical occupations must be given a central position so that children can understand the social and human context in which new inventions and discoveries arose, and upon which are based the intellectual theories and spiritual ideals of adult life. It is only with the perspective gained in the early years that children and youth can later engage in more distinctive preparation of a vocational nature and see its place in the whole circle of human activities. By seeing any vocation in its relationships with the other aspects of adult activities, the standard of social value can be applied to the calling in a complete way and its isolation from the life of the child, and from the spiritual life of adults, can be overcome.

W. T. HARRIS AND TRADITIONAL EDUCATION

Harris's Views

There is a sense in which the above caption is incongruous. For W. T. Harris, as an Hegelian, was opposed to the position which conceived of education as a process of passive absorption on the part of the learner. He specifically rejected faculty psychology because this theory did not account for the genesis of the higher powers of the intellect and the will out of

the lower powers of feeling and their reaction to transform the latter. Furthermore, he strenuously objected to an education that ignored the educative influence of social institutions other than the school. To the extent, then, that traditional educational practices promoted passivity in learning, the sharpening of the higher faculties, and the individual focus, W. T. Harris cannot be placed in the traditional camp.

But there is another sense in which Harris and the traditional school are intimately linked, with Harris, at most, being merely a vitalizing influence in a rationalization of the usual practices. It is in this sense that Dewey sees Harris in his review of the latter's book *Psychologic Foundations of Education*.[33] As Dewey explains it, Harris has on one hand an active individual striving to reproduce the form, and participate in, the content of the absolute personality; out of feeling, the individual comes to consciousness of his end, self-development; out of feeling arises finally intellect and will. On the other hand, there are the institutions of society which alone enable the individual to realize his capacities. Some of these institutions, the family, civil society, and the state, have for their end the satisfaction of man's physical being and minister to the lower states of feeling. Other institutions, of art, of religion, and of science, tend to elevate the natural, or feeling, self into a spiritual life of intellect and will and into participation in the life of the social whole.

The school, for Harris, serves to supply the individual with the tools with which he will observe and understand the institutions around him. There are three stages in this development. There is the kindergarten period where objects and images are used as symbols of universals and ideals. In the second, or elementary, stage, the individual must master the conventionalities of human learning—reading, writing, and arithmetic. In the third period, of secondary and higher education, the individual is able to see the functions of all branches of learning in the totality of spiritual experience. With the tools he has learned to use, the bits of knowledge he has acquired can be converted into wisdom.

In each stage of learning there is a common framework of subject-matter, consisting of five coordinate groups of study corresponding to the five windows of the soul that look out upon the five great divisions in the life of man. These divisions are: the formal aspect of nature represented by physics and mathematics; the active scene of nature shown by natural history, biology, or geography; the will of mankind seen in history; the intellect seen in language and grammar; and the inner life of aspiration and ideal represented in literature.

Now, while Harris's psychology may represent some advance over passive or faculty psychology, Dewey still does not like it. Even so, he might not call Harris "traditional" on that ground. It is, rather, in Harris's ethics, wherein he accepts the age-old separation of the spiritual from the physical realm, that the ground is located for including him among the traditionalists in education.

Dewey's Criticism

Aside from the fact that Dewey objects to the psychology, the difficulty he has with Harris's views is at the point of separation of the spiritual and the physical, and the division of institutions into those that are moral and which have a spiritual function and those nonmoral activities that serve only physical needs.

And while, superficially considered, industrial society might be regarded simply as a mechanism for contributing to the physical comfort and well-being of man; more deeply considered, invention and commerce are chief instrumentalities which spiritual culture has had to rely upon for its general propagation and diffusion.[34]

Dewey agrees that Harris presents a fair statement of existing practices, but deplores the fact that he lends his status in the

educational world in support of this traditional concept of education. He says:

That the period of elementary education shall long continue to be regarded as centering about the technical symbols of intercommunication, eked out with fragmentary bits of information concerning the world of nature and of man, seems to me incredible. All that is most vital and progressive in existing elementary education is moving away from these traditions, in the direction of introducing positive and first-hand contact with the realities of experience, as distinct from the mere symbols of knowledge, and toward more positive spiritual content.[35]

As for Harris's notion of secondary or higher education and its relationship with the earlier stages, Dewey objects on both psychological and ethical grounds. For Dewey, learning does not take place by starting with particulars that will lead to generalizations when the intellect begins to function at the time of higher learning. Instead, even as Harris suggests, only to ignore, the early phase of mind is synthetic rather than analytic.[36] "Instead of going from particulars through interrelations up to wholes, the mind moves from the apprehension of vague wholes, through correlative specifications and generalization, to systematized wholes." [37] But the postponement of a focus in education upon wholes, upon generalizations and relationships, is even more objectionable on moral grounds, as Dewey emphasizes in this statement:

It would be intolerable in a democratic country to have ninety-five per cent of children shut off for the most part from ethical content and from the influences which tend to convert information into wisdom, reserving this latter just for the elite who are able to go to college.[38]

Dewey appreciates greatly Harris's emphasis upon the educative influences of social institutions. Their difference on this point is that Harris is still an Hegelian; he is intent on filling an individual consciousness with the content of the universal consciousness. Dewey's notion of activity is no longer

that of the individual appropriating for himself the products
of the Absolute as embodied in institutions; instead, he thinks
of human beings as creators and controllers of their institutions. He says:

> While it is impossible to overestimate the spiritual dependence of
> the individual upon society, does not Dr. Harris somewhat ignore
> the extent to which democratic society, with the resources of
> modern science at command, can put into the hands of the indi-
> vidual the *methods* by which the spiritual interests of society are
> conserved, and thus emancipate him very largely from the necessity
> of immediate dependence upon its *products*? If this be true,
> would not practical acquaintance with processes, even from the
> very first, demand relatively a larger sphere of importance as com-
> pared with information about products? [39]

Thus, the traditionalism that Dewey sees in Harris's plan of
education is not that of the still current passive psychology, nor
that of the conservatism that ignored the effects of social
institutions on human personality, but that of the age-old
separation of the child from the adult world and the division
of the adult world into separate spiritual and physical realms.
Harris's scheme would perpetuate the very problem the solution of which Dewey saw as the primary function of education
for his time. It is inconceivable for Dewey that institutions
of the family, civil society, and the state contribute only by
necessity to the elevation of the spiritual life; nor would he
permit the institutions of art, of religion, and of science to
make mere ethical judgments *about* the former institutions.
For Dewey, all the institutions of men participate in the moral
life and are to be judged by their contributions to that life.
Nor is this enough; for him, the highest ethical principle
demands that each person share in the creation and control of
the institutions whose functions are to achieve the highest
ethical ends of humanity. Dewey opposes any education that is
traditional in the sense that it permits only part of the people
to share merely in the products of the good life.

VII

THE THEORY OF SCHOOLING

THE PROBLEM OF EDUCATION

"FIRST IN IMPORTANCE is the conception of the *problem* of education."[1] Dewey made this statement in 1936, in an appendix to the account of the Dewey School prepared by Mayhew and Edwards. He was discussing the bearing of his philosophic theory upon education. He said that the experiences of thirty years might conceivably have colored the original theory. But it seems obvious that as he reflected on his own developmental thought, he saw it as a process of problemizing and hypothesizing for the solution of the problem he formulated. The importance he claims for the function of a problem as his guide for the development of his philosophic and educational theorizing seems clearly evident upon examination of that development.

The preceding chapters have recorded attempts to clarify the tentative and reconstructed aspects of his thought one by one. But it is a mistake to think of Dewey's own method as one which led him to apply his psychological ideas to education only after he had worked with and reshaped these ideas. Nor would it seem accurate to hold that after satisfying himself with regard to psychological theory and its meaning for education, he then took up the study of logical, or of ethical, theory, and similarly followed such a process. Now it may be conceded that he did not develop his views of the basic human disciplines independently of each other. It may be clear that, though he focused on one, he constantly referred each developing set of ideas to the others until he had shaped them all into a consistent and interrelated system of ideas. But it would still be misleading to hold that after accomplishing this he then turned to the task of applying these interrelated sets of ideas to matters educational in import. The highly significant place of the *problem* of education as the guide for his developmental thought would be overlooked. He claims the conception of the problem was first in importance. The record of his intellectual development supports this insistence.

It should be sufficient to point to his own interrelated theories for the clue to his method. By his psychology, his spring to action was in impulse as an active being. By his ethics, he exercised his specific functions in specific surroundings. His logic suggests that in doing so he encountered difficulties and doubts, eventually of great magnitude. The general nature of these doubts is perhaps suggested by his two early papers of the 1880's, "The Ethics of Science" and "The Ethics of Democracy." Science and democracy seemed to hold great possibilities for himself and others in their efforts to exercise specific function in specific situations, that is, for the development of individuality. But the hopes were not being realized. Something was amiss, but what was the problem? His inquiry, by his own theory, took him back and forth from a tentative formulation of the problem, as in his earlier idealist period, to the reexamination of the basic human disciplines, to a reformulation of the problem and to tentative hypotheses for its solution. A more settled problem of great magnitude emerged. He saw it fundamentally as a problem of education. An hypothesis of equally many faceted dimensions developed as the solution for the problem. Thus, Dewey's educational theory perhaps can be more clearly understood if it is seen as an hypothesis for the solution of a problem. He held foremost in mind the problem, he says, as he derived the educational practices of the Dewey School from the same theories that also formulated the problem. Quest for clarity regarding the meaning of his ideas should be advanced if the significance of the place of the problem in his thought is kept centrally in mind.

But what is *the* problem? After stating that the conception of the problem was first in importance he went on to say, "In substance this problem is the harmonizing of individual traits with social ends and values."[2] Following the suggestions just made as to Dewey's method, this may come as something of a shock. For the outcome of this method may seem to be no more than the ready-made, age-old problem of the relation of the individual to the group. But it is the same old problem in a very general sense only. For Dewey, at least, saw it as "an ever re-newed problem, one which each new generation has to solve over again for itself."[3] Since we know that for him a problem is well on its way to solution when it is well formulated, this means that each generation has to reformulate the problem as well as to solve it over again for itself.

Dewey's own definition of the problem is to be found throughout his writings. In the context in which he stated it as the harmonizing of individual traits with social ends and values, he was writing briefly and in nontechnical language. Actually, this statement does not indicate the problem for his generation, but merely recognizes a generalized version of a goal for any generation. He made no attempt here to restate the way he saw this goal nor did he point to the difficulties standing in the way of its attainment. We have already had opportunity to receive impressions of his conception of the problem from the papers we have examined for other purposes. But it should be helpful to concentrate briefly on what he saw as the difficulties, and how he viewed the goal. This requires an examination of his diagnosis of the social situation in which his generation is to reformulate and resolve the problem.

That Dewey saw cultural change amounting to revolution as characteristic of his own society is clear, even though he did not give a great deal of explicit attention to an analysis of the social situation in the papers we have examined.[4] Nevertheless, scattered throughout these papers are numerous descriptions of the social scene that point up his assessment of the current conditions.[5] We have noted that he saw science and technology as the forces creating rapid and widespread changes in social life. There were now minute divisions of labor and increasing specialization in the production, processing, and distribution of goods and services. Not only were the latter being supplied, as necessities, more abundantly than ever before envisioned; they were creating hosts of new material wants and desires. The family which had formerly been both a producing and consuming unit, and as such was in close contact with the actualities of the physical world, was now losing its direct producing function. Only one member of the family, perhaps, was sharing but an infinitesimal part of a tremendously complex and interdependent process of production. This newer industrial arrangement was tending to destroy the older form of simple, rural community life with its face-to-face personal relationships, supplanting this with the urbanization of the population and its impersonal network of relationships. Both this impersonal aspect of many of the daily activities of life and the extreme specialization in occupations led to the development of many subgroups held together by some common vocational or social interest.

We have previously noted that Dewey saw much that was good in these changes. In addition to the good resulting from the vastly increased productive power and the relief of drudgery through the use of machines, he recognized many other compensating factors that held great promise for the development of enriched and varied personalities. In spite of these advantages, we have seen that Dewey felt the great rapidity and the ramifications of change were causing the educational problem of harmonizing individual traits with social ends and values to be increasingly difficult to meet. We have observed his concern over the effect of minute specialization of occupation on the life of the child. The latter was losing firsthand contact with physical actualities, and was being deprived of the opportunity for disciplinary training in responsible and char-

acter building activities carried on within the home. The child was being forced to live in an unreal and irresponsible world of his own, separated from any vital relationships with adult social purposes and interests.

The same specialization, he thought, was also fragmentizing the adult world. It was becoming more and more difficult for adults to see the place and meaning of their daily work and activities within the larger context of interdependent productive arrangements and intricate human relationships. Since economic life was not democratized, and yet was being increasingly interwoven with all aspects of social and political life, the democratic achievements in these areas were in danger of being lost.

The fact that men, unable to anchor their daily concerns to the wider social arrangements, sought some measure of security through membership in subgroups heightened the possibility of significant conflict among diverse groups. Dewey saw no inherent harm in these groups; there was potential good in the enriched alternatives they developed. But he was greatly concerned over the conditions under which conflicts took place and the methods used to resolve them. Unless conflict was met with free and open inquiry on the part of all individuals concerned, there was grave danger of either chaos or the imposition by the stronger groups of their particular ways and beliefs upon the weaker. The harmonious development of individual traits with social ends and values would become impossible in both cases.

Not only were men trying to establish a sense of belonging through membership in subgroups; they were also compartmentalizing various aspects of their individual lives. Since often they could not see the meaning of their work or calling in relation to the wider social life, they were increasingly looking upon their occupations as necessary evils to submit to daily, after which they could really live. This, for Dewey, was an extension of the age-old separation of the meanly physical from the ethical and spiritual; but now, he felt, it was inconceivable that the elaborate processes of abundant production of material goods should remain apart from functioning ethical considerations. Furthermore, while in earlier times the work of supplying necessities was considered outside the ethical realm, in fact some ethical qualities prevailed in pride in workmanship as the artisan created his product; but in the modern machine age, under prevailing conditions, even this guiding ethic was lost.

Perhaps the most disturbing effect upon social conditions resulting from the development of science, in Dewey's belief, was the separation of this science from common sense. Formerly, common sense may have been uncommonly common, but it *was* common. Children and adults shared a world of joys and sufferings, a world of particular and concrete situations, of obstacles, frustrations, and struggles. But science now had brought forth a new world of generalizations, of statistical averages, of mathematical laws, and the more this new world was proclaimed the "real" world the more the common sense world of particular experiences faded away into a welter of subjective ideas that left individual traits lost—wandering aimlessly somewhere below the new world of science posited as "real." The ends and values of society had grown out of the common sense world of trials and tribulations. But now the inhabitants of this world shared, at best, only in the ultimate products of science, while the methods of science were rapidly becoming a function of experts. These products of science were upsetting and changing the conditions of men's struggles, and were disturbing the values permeating their experiences. It was becoming increasingly difficult to harmonize individual traits with changing social conditions and values when men did not consciously share in the processes which were creating these changes.

Science was not simply disturbing the older system of values; it was extending the separation between the physical and

spiritual worlds—it was tending to separate itself from the realm of ethics. Other than commitment to the method itself, science was considered sound to the extent that it eliminated values. As Dewey saw it, with science and technology creating a marvelous new world of material wonders, to continue to exile this world from the ethical realm implied the possible destruction of the spiritual life by an onrushing materialism. In this situation, the individual was being forced to choose between the life of the senses and the life of the spirit, or, to compartmentalize the two realms of experience in order to escape complete disharmony between his everyday interests and concerns on the one hand, and social ends and values on the other. More and more the individual tended to be lost in a feeling of helplessness and irresponsibility.

THE REQUIREMENT OF SCHOOLING

One way of summing up what Dewey saw as the difficulties preventing the harmonizing of individual traits with social ends and values is to say that they were barriers breaking the continuity of experience. The difficulties were the obstacles to full and free mediation of impulse. We have seen that, for Dewey, man is an active being. Impulse is primary; it encounters obstacles of the natural surroundings and conflicts with the social surroundings. Man is capable of realizing his wants and powers with reference to these peculiar surroundings. To the degree that he mediates any single impulse with all other experiences he not only satisfies his own potential for individuality but contributes to the collective well being of a community of persons of which he is a member. But what if there are barriers, not to impulses, but to their full and free mediation? These would prevent attainment of either value. There were these obstacles that broke the continuity of experience. There were gaps, or separations, in experience and they were increasing. We have just noted some of them. There was a growing gap in family life between productive functions and other experiences; the isolation of much of child life from adult experiences; the separation of adult productive functions from other adult interests and concerns; divisions among adults into groups shut off from full and free communication with each other; growing psychological barriers between the physical aspects of life and the spiritual; separation of the origins of problems in common sense from their solution by experts; a gap between the ethical method of science and its nonethical functions.

A problem exists when the barriers to the attainment of a goal are defined. The notion of gaps in experience seems to represent the difficulties for Dewey. But the goal, too, needs specification. One thing the goal of harmony of individual traits with social ends and values does not mean is absence of conflict. On the contrary, conflict is essential for the development of individuality. There can be no full and free mediation of impulse without obstacles confronting it, either from within the individual or from the rest of the situation. In fact, even deliberate search for trouble, for doubts, seems to be required if man is more and more to realize his possibilities. Harmony, then, put negatively, is not the absence of conflict but the absence of barriers to the complete mediation of conflict. Positively, harmony is a resolution of conflict that satisfies the individual and the community of persons of which he is a member. The degree of harmony depends upon the methods by which this resolution is achieved. Science and democracy are the best available methods by which man can overcome the obstacles of the natural world and resolve the conflicts of the social world. With these instruments to aid man as he exercises his specific functions even by searching out obstacles and conflicts in his specific surroundings, and with the latter being relatively limitless, then man's potentiality for development of individuality is similarly limitless.

This suggests the crux of the significance of *the* problem

for Dewey's generation. The acuteness of the problem did not reside so much in the fact that established social rules prevented the freedom of individual expressions of valued wants. Perhaps this had been the case in many generations and harmony of sorts had been found in some wishful anticipation of a millennium or in a blind resignation to conditions apparently necessary. But now science and democracy were creating new visions of man's potential for individuality and were available as instruments for its development. The tragedy lay in the fact that these same instruments, or perhaps truncated conceptions of them, were creating also the growing gaps in experience that represented the obstacles standing in the way of this expanding vision of the goal and its attainment.

The problem, then, is how to overcome the gaps in experience. Experience, for Dewey, is education; hence, it is a problem of education. If experiences did not suffer these discontinuities they would simply grow and develop in life. Since they do, however, a conscious and deliberate effort is required to provide the conditions for continuity, or for overcoming the separations in experience. Part, at least, of this conscious and deliberate effort is provided by schooling. Thus schooling takes on significance in proportion to the lack of these conditions in social life.

In the preceding chapter we examined current educational movements and Dewey's reactions to them. The Herbartians, the Child Study Groups, the Manual Training Movement, and W. T. Harris all represented trends in the "Newer Education." One sense of their "newness" probably rested upon the conception on the part of their adherents of a growing significance for schooling somewhat similar to Dewey's. These people, too, seemed to feel that everyday experiences in social life were not adequately building individuality or a stable social order. In this situation schooling had to contribute more than the mere periphery of character supplied by the "older" schooling. But while this may be so, Dewey, we saw, was dissatisfied with these movements. For their practices, rather than bridging the gaps in experience, were often serving to widen the separations.

Educational practices are always derived from some, even unconsciously held, theories. Errors in practice suggest, then, inadequacies of theory. From Dewey's point of view there may have been any or all of three types of inadequacies in the theories underlying these movements. In the first place, the theories may have developed without reference to the problem, or even a problem, of education. Thus, they provided no adequate guide to the resolution of the doubts from which they sprang. Secondly, any one leg of the theoretical foundations of the practices in these movements may not have shown the possibilities for the solution of the problem as Dewey defined it. On the contrary, they may have shown gaps in experience as inherent in human behavior or social organization. In the third place, even if one leg showed such possibilities, other aspects of theoretical foundation for these practices may either have been inconsistent or neglected. This one-sided base would lead to the kind of confusion where attempts to bridge one gap would only serve to widen another.

It may be useful here to take a second look at some of Dewey's specific criticisms of the movements. In doing so, we may see more clearly, perhaps, the faithfulness of his later claim that the *problem* was first in importance. For as he weighed these movements it seems apparent that his measure was the extent to which each showed the theoretical possibilities for the solution of the problem of education—for overcoming the separations in experience.

For example, we have seen that what disturbed Dewey about Harris's theories was the latter's insistence that, on one hand, there were social institutions ministering to the individual's lower states of feeling and, on the other, that there were institutions of a higher ethical nature serving to elevate the spiritual life of man. Dewey objected to this division of the self into a lower sphere of feeling and desire and a

higher area of intellect and will; he objected to the separation of ethical social institutions from those conceived as necessary, but meanly practical. Education, he felt, was the struggle to overcome these very disunities. In Harris's scheme of schooling, Dewey rejected the emphasis on the products of man's endeavors at the expense of denying a place for participation in the processes through which these products came to be. We noted also that Dewey was most unhappy because Harris separated schooling into stages wherein the earlier ones focused merely upon, for Harris, the nonethical lower states of feeling, as well as upon only the form or acquisition of the tools of learning, and reserved for later stages attention to the ethical content of higher concerns of life and the development of wisdom. Among other difficulties this meant, for Dewey, that schooling would not serve the great majority of children who, because of social conditions, as well as the debilitating effect of their experiences in the earlier stages of schooling, would never participate in the later phases where they were expected to develop wisdom and ethical character.

In regard to the Manual Training Movement, we have seen that Dewey deplored the sharp distinction between the life of work and the work of life. In schooling, he objected to emphasis upon manual work as either mere busy-work or as only of strictly utilitarian concern. He could not agree to a division of the curriculum into vocational studies and the scholastic subjects. In fact, he pointed out that it was the very cleft between the material and spiritual interests of man that schooling should attempt to overcome. In order to bridge this gap, he favored vocational work in schooling not as a distinct but as an integral part of the curriculum. This central position of occupations was necessary, he felt, because the modern child entered a world of complex, technical, mechanical, and intellectual devices and resources, and schooling must meet the problem of establishing vital connections of these adult products and processes with the life of the immature child.

Dewey saw the Child Study Movement, with all its faults, as signifying the importance of schooling. He noted that schooling becomes acutely necessary at times of great agitation and change in social life. One interest in the child stems from the insight that social life can be controlled and orderly if the child is prepared to take his place in accord with the ends and values of society. Another interest in schooling comes from the view of the child as an individual with great potentialities for varied expressions of personality. Dewey suggested that rather than choosing either of these one-sided interests, schooling must be the attempt to meet the problem of reconciling and achieving both.

We have seen that Dewey agreed with the Herbartians that schooling must seek to develop moral character, and to attain this end it must focus from the beginning on a concentrated ethical content and not merely on the form or tools of learning. But he pointed out that this focus must not be on content as the products of social life but that the processes by which the products had been achieved must be included. To take the child, interested in the social activities about him, and expect him to attain moral character through the proper presentation of the ethical content of social products is to omit the needed link between these end points. This link is the child's own effort to realize his ideas within his surroundings. Furthermore, as Dewey saw it, the Herbartians erred in their attempt to select the content of schooling by seeking the correspondence between the child's interests at various stages and the cultural epochs from lower to higher. This not only applied a false standard for the latter classification but it also tended to shut off the child from the vital concerns of present life. It was, he thought, the relations of the child's interests with the present social situation which schooling should seek to clarify. The need for a criterion for the selection of subject-matter could be much better served, in his opinion, if the Herbartians

would look for a pattern of activities to which ethical content accrued. Dewey found this pattern, as we know, in the typical occupations of man.

THE REQUIREMENTS FOR EDUCATIONAL THEORY

The trend of these criticisms seems clear. When seen together, they unite in a recurrent theme which confirms the statement made by Dewey in 1936 regarding the importance of the problem of education. His objections to the theoretical guides for these various educational movements indicate that, as he saw it, they did not meet the requirements for educational theory. These requirements are now evident. Put simply, there must be a problem; this must show the desired goal and the difficulties standing in the way of its attainment. This must be a problem defined with reference to the basic human disciplines and thus multidimensional. A problem well defined must show possibilities for solution; hence, the disciplines pointing to the problem must be so conceptualized as in their interrelationships consistently to support this possibility. They must provide an equally many faceted hypothesis that can serve as a guide to its test in educational practice.

These requirements may be "simply put"; but they are tremendous in their implications. They emphasize the magnitude of the task Dewey set for himself. One may well ask what sustained him in his great effort to show that the gaps in experience were practical and institutional, not theoretical. After all, many respected theories of psychology, logic, ethics, and social philosophy had long supported the view of discontinuities being inherent in individual and social experience. Some significant idea must have sustained him in his search for the theoretical possibility of continuity in experience.

Probably this sustaining conception was the notion of viewing from the standpoint of humanity. This means seeing life as a common struggle of all humanity to build human beings in an humane social order. For Dewey, this idea came from no traumatic vision; it came from his reading of the accomplishments of science. Among its various phases, science is analysis; it describes and explains. It also is experimental; it predicts and controls. Scientists had, among their subject-matters, studied the preconceived ideas and institutions of men, examining in minute detail their origin and evolution. This scientific analysis had finally disclosed an underlying unity within the disunity of conventions and customs; it had come upon "humanity" itself. It had shown that men's ideas and institutions had evolved in a long struggle and conflict with the forces of a world with rather narrow and rigid limitations. As men sought their advantage within these limitations they became inventive with respect to the physical world and legislative in regard to the social world. Early, they saw the need for systematic control of social legislation and of invention, but they had no method for realizing this demand. Consequently invention remained haphazard and social control customary and improvised. But now science had developed as a method of invention and as a motor for social control. It would serve these functions provided an appropriate perspective, supported by analysis and adequate to guide its application and development, was not overlooked or ignored. For, by disclosing unity in a common humanity, scientific analysis gave evidence of and support for the ethical conception that all men should share in the ends and values of society, and, more important, that each must share in the creation and control of the processes that achieve these ends, and, finally, that in such participation each individual best realizes his own potentialities.

If once this standpoint is taken, science can clarify its methods for the work of synthesizing knowledge and shaping it for its use in systematic invention and social control. This standpoint is the common inheritance of the present generation

from the joys and sufferings of previous generations; for it to be consciously shared, a wide distribution of intelligence is also required, an intelligence imbued with this perspective and developed as an instrument of scientific control. The task of building such intelligence is the work of education. In order for education to fulfill this function, the prior disclosures of scientific analysis must be selected and interpreted for their bearing upon the function assigned to education. The science which was creating the critical gaps in experience and thus precipitating the problem of education in its current form could also provide the insights and methods necessary for overcoming these separations. What is proposed is no Hegelian movement of ideas with men merely the pawns of evolving ideas; what is proposed is a controlled and deliberate search by men who had come to see human problems from the standpoint of humanity.

This, then, may have been the idea sustaining Dewey in the task of fulfilling his rigorous requirements for educational theory. A second look at his reconstruction of the basic human disciplines of psychology, logic, ethics, and social philosophy may serve to make clearer how both this sustaining idea and what he saw as requirements for educational theory guided him in his inquiry. With these ideas held centrally in mind, brief reexamination of his efforts to reinterpret these disciplines may reveal them in operation.

THE BASIC HUMAN DISCIPLINES AS FOUNDATIONS FOR A THEORY OF SCHOOLING

Psychology

The view that sees human nature as moved to act by the feeling or idea that comes with an impression from an outside object only lends support to already acute separations in experience. An object impinges, man feels or gets an idea, he acts. Was his act successful or satisfying or good? For all we can tell it merely subsides until a second object impinges; sensation, thought, and action reside in separate realms. Furthermore, each thought or act is isolated from others; sustained or connected thought and action depend upon the continuous and related impressions received from without. With increasing practical and institutional divisions and barriers among men and their activities, this psychology would hardly suggest the possibility for harmony either within the individual or between him and others.

Similarly the view that human nature, through sensation and feeling, is stirred to self-consciousness which by means of the intellect and will strives to realize a universal consciousness also supports gaps in experience. Since the individual is a finite being, he can never bridge the gap to the universal consciousness; he can only strive. Furthermore, the intellect and will, after being awakened by feelings of joy or sorrow, sever partnership with these lower states and henceforth seek only to restrict their functions to their necessary but unworthy sphere. And, finally, the individual will can only hope to reproduce the universal intellect and will, not to participate in its determination or control. If gaps exist between the universal and its embodiment in the world of man, the individual has no way of overcoming them.

The difficulties in these views can be met if one starts with action itself as primary. Man is a creature of impulse; he is already acting and always acting toward some content. Since the world is, indeed, finite, man meets obstacles to the expression of his impulses. Since the world is inhabited, but not by the individual alone, he encounters conflict with others as they seek to realize their impulses. Consequently he must mediate his impulses with these obstacles and conflicts. Within the process of mediation arise emotion, interest, and reflective thought, which serve to sustain and direct his further actions.

Much of this process goes on in his imagination as he develops his ends and purposes in relation to their means of attainment; thus his action can be undertaken deliberately, even though its origin is in impulse. Since the impulse always has a content, some "object" of the physical or social world, there is no psychological necessity for gaps between the development of individual traits and the physical realities or social ideals. And since the impulse is primary for both children and adults, there is no necessary gap that places the child in a feeling world and the adult in an intellectual and willing world; the process of mediation is the same, the difference being only in the context in which the mediation occurs.

Logic

If it is man's best, most fruitful, and productive method of thought that is widening the gaps in his experiences, gaps which are making it increasingly difficult to harmonize individual traits with social ends and values, then it is advantageous to know what that method is in order that it might be put to work in breaking down these separations which its limited application has engendered. To view thought as mere manipulation of abstractions from an already divided sensory content would not serve to unite this material; such a logic could only show consistency and noncontradiction; it could not rework the content of experience in any way to harmonize individual and group experiences. And even if thought is concerned with the actual data of the senses, to the extent that it accepts this material ready-made, such thought can only rearrange and organize its data; it can not control or change it to effect harmony and unity of experience. And finally, if thought is nothing but an attempt to imitate or reinstate a fixed, complete, and universal "thought," it can, at best, only serve to get in step with all the existing gaps in experience.

To hold any of these views of logic is but to support separations of abstractions from realities, thought from content or action, and ideals from existential conditions. But if thought is viewed as a process of inquiry, starting from doubt or uncertainty, the very function of thought becomes that of completing a unity of experience, to effect a consummatory closure in experience, and thus to eliminate or overcome separations in any phase of the process. This view of thought actually coincides with the scientific thinking that was making the problem of education critical. Instead of separating the scientific manner of thought from the common sense problems of men, it should be put to work there. When so generalized, the life of reflection becomes continuous with man's attempt to realize his best capabilities in the social-natural matrix of his life. Furthermore, if thought is an instrument for gathering data relevant to a confronting problem, for formulating them into considered plans of action, and for guiding and testing those plans in action, there can be no valid separation of thought from action. Hence, such a view supports the continuity of individual and social ends and purposes with the processes by which they are to be realized, and such continuity is in effect a denial of the separation of "physical" means from "spiritual" ideals.

Ethics

The view that judges an act good because its outcome results in a pleasant state of feeling for the individual actor gives no help in unifying an individual's traits among themselves or with those of others. Indeed, it makes each act completely separate and dependent upon isolated states of feeling and suggests no way at all of guiding these actions toward social ends and values. Nor does it help to judge the act in consequence of its contribution to the general welfare, if at the same time it is held that the individual is psychologically

moved to act by the pleasure motive. For this merely emphasizes the gap between the individual's pleasure and the pleasure of all. It affords no clue for harmonizing the former with the latter. To say that it is self-evident that one is morally bound to consider another's welfare, instead of supplying a link between individual and social welfare, merely separates general welfare as an abstraction from the concrete welfare of another person; for one's own feeling of pleasure will not inform him of the pleasure of another in a particular situation. Furthermore, if the last fact is conceded, and it is said that it is not necessary to know another's pleasure because the attainment by each individual of his own good will add up to the general good, we have not only the illogical proposition that because each man wants happiness for himself he therefore wants all men to be happy, but also the admission that there is no reality in the actual relations between individual and social welfare.

If the attempt to judge the quality of acts merely in terms of their consequences fails to guide individual traits toward social ends and values, it might be that the view that judges action in terms of the motives of the actor may succeed. But immediately the difficulty begins anew; for now there is no source for the motive—no spring to action. Even if it is said, either logically or illogically, that the individual does act and is guided by his motive, then each act has an independent motive and can be judged only by that motive. Each prompting is absolute, and thus must contradict some other equally absolute motive. Such a view not only fails to harmonize individual traits among themselves but most certainly cannot achieve their unity with social motives.

The judgment of the quality of an act either by its consequences or by the motive of the actor supports the very gaps that must be overcome. Furthermore, limitation of ethical judgment to judgment of an act after the fact involves a separation of judgment from the act and affords no direction

to any given act nor continuity to a succession of acts. Therefore, the criterion must be found within, not outside, the
process of acting. An act involves both subject and object, or
better, an individual in a concrete situation. The person acting seeks to realize his traits as an individual within some
particular situation. The situation, taken in its fullness, is a
community of persons. As the individual seeks to satisfy his
impulses he must mediate any impulse with his other experiences and with the experiences of others. The completest
possible interaction of all these experiences is the best assurance
that the performance of his specific functions will realize his
wants and powers in harmony with the specific situation. Thus
the ideal that guides behavior and the criterion of the value
of any act is the ideal and criterion of education, and the
practical problem of education is the equivalent of the moral
problem.

This ethical standpoint lends firm moral support to the task
of overcoming the critically growing gaps in experience. The
situations in which the child must function are preeminently
social situations in which adult functions and interests shape
and direct experiences with which the child must mediate his
impulses. The dominant adult interests and activities are their
occupations. Since these are becoming highly specialized and
since they are permeated with adult ideals of art and science
and values, they are highly complex. Yet the guidance of the
child's conduct toward the completest possible interaction of
his interests within specific occupational situations will tend
toward the unity of child and adult worlds. Furthermore, this
view relates the moral with the intellectual since intelligence
is brought to bear in placing any act within the widest context
of experience. This means, further, that science and its methods
are relied upon to modify judgments of ways to act in common
sense situations. And, finally, within the process, commencing
with individual biological, physical needs and closing with
shared consummation and realization, is included the media-

tion of material demands, emotional commitments, and the highest spiritual ideals of society.

Social Philosophy

The democratic view which holds that all men must share in the ethical ends and values of society does not serve adequately to harmonize those products with the processes of development of individual traits. For this is a partial idea of democracy. Being one-sided, it supports the separation of the good life as a product from the processes of living the good life. It divides political life from social, economic, and industrial life; it divides the governors from the governed; it separates the common will from the formation and expression of that will; it sets apart the emotional and material demands of the people from the intellectual and spiritual creations of their leaders. In short, this partial view of democracy supports the very gaps that must be overcome because it separates the ends of society from social participation in the means of their attainment. Even aristocracy may claim that all men share in the glorious achievements of the ruler.

The complete democratic view which will support the practices necessary to develop unity of individual traits with social ends and values must include the idea that all men must share in the creation of the good life. The development of human personality, the exercise of man's specific functions, is his end, and he must work out this end in specific situations in harmony with the developing personalities of others. Personality is the end and as end resides equally in each individual and each must be free to initiate and follow from within his ideal. In this pursuit he must participate with others in the development of a common will, in the expression of that will, and in its control and execution in behalf of personality, which is as universal as humanity.

In this view the child is seen as a developing child personality, sharing in the growth of adult personalities, with the gap between them only in degree, not in kind. And this gap can be seen closing through the participation of the child's specific functions in social situations guided and mediated by adult functions and interests. Through this participation in the intimate personal relationships of his early social situation in life, the child develops a perspective of the typical adult interests and the ends and values that permeate them. In his later years, with the growing exercise of his functions, he shares more and more in the control of these interests and in the formulation and judgment of goals and practices. His growing intelligence, with the help of the methods of science, guides him, through experimental means, toward the realization of his impulses and the satisfaction of his physical and emotional needs with due reference to the widest context of experience, which is to say, toward the highest ethical standard. Hence, the complete democratic view that all men must share in the creation and control of the means necessary for the best development of individual traits locates in the creative quality of this process the means for overcoming the gaps in experience; for the apparent entities separated by these gaps, the child and the adult, common sense and science, the physical and the ideal, are merely end points of this process.

THE FUNDAMENTALS OF DEWEY'S THEORY OF SCHOOLING

Education, Dewey has said, is all one with living; education is experience; it is growth. These familiar expressions signify the movement and outcome of the process of living. The two factors of this process are "an immature, undeveloped being; and certain social aims, meanings, values incarnate in the matured experiences of the adult. The educative process is the due interaction of these forces." [6] It is a process in which an active being seeks to express his impulses within surroundings the significance of which stems from the expressions of other impulsive beings. This sharing of expressions consti-

tutes experiences, where each being acts toward others and undergoes their actions toward him. This interaction gives rise to conflict. Because of intercommunication through language, thought arises and guides choices in modes of expression. Thus the possibilities of growth in the meaning of experiences are infinitely varied and tremendous.

While the potentiality for this growth in experience is great, the conditions under which experience is had may be such as to restrict the possibilities and stunt growth. The process of living, then, which is all one with education, may be either desirable or undesirable, good or bad. It is unnecessary to repeat that when, as in this period, social conditions lead to undesirable experience, the educative process needs conscious and deliberate attention, and schooling is devised as a means of providing desirable experiences. Good experiences are growing experiences, not in the sense of mere accumulation, but "growing" in the sense of "expanding in meaning and significance." The terms growth and expansion imply continuity; therefore the meaning of any experience must grow out of a former, and lead into a subsequent, experience. It is this factor of continuity, so lacking in education, that must be supplied by schooling. Thus schooling is education in a narrower sense than the total process of living; it cannot encompass education in this wider sense of total experience. But it can and should contribute to the continuity of experience together with all that is implied in the term with respect to growth.

Schooling, or the narrower education, then, begins with individuals already participating in the wider educative process. From the consequent experiences, had primarily in family life situations, children have acquired needs and interests and modes of expression with which their later experiences in school must be continuous. These needs, interests, and modes of expression serve, then, as the starting point of the process of schooling. The fact that this process is a conscious and deliberate effort implies that it is guided by individuals who serve in the conditions for continuous growth of experiences. Since the possibilities of growth, as already suggested, are almost infinitely varied, the full limits being unknown by the guides or teachers, there can be no fixed end to the process; the end can only be further growth. But the teachers can and should know the best evidences of growth which have accrued to the past and present experiences of others. It is from knowledge of these expressions and their meanings that the teacher can interpret the present needs, interests, and expressions of children and guide them in subsequent experiences which add meaning and lead on to still further significance.

Growth leading to further growth depends upon the quality of the mediation of impulses in the specific context of any given experience. To speak of any given experience is to indicate that total experience consists of a related, and thus continuous, series of singular experiences, each with a beginning and end. But continuity refers not only to the relations of one experience to another; it also signifies the integration of the three phases of any complete experience, namely, thought, feeling, and action. Mediated experience starts from impulse arising out of particular situations; any impulse must be referred to others and to the specific surroundings; it must be sustained by feeling, guided by thought, and consummated in action; an experience is continuous if it leads to subsequent experience in still wider situations. The teachers or guides to this continuity of the experiences of students must lead in supplying the wider situations by contributing their more expansive experiences and by using these to interpret what meanings they hold which are continuous with the present experiences of the students.

The context of any meaningful experience is ultimately a social situation. Teachers guiding the having of experiences, then, must see to it that this social quality pervades the process

of development of impulse through the interchange of expressions of each individual engaged in the process of living in the school. Included is the teacher as representative of the wider social experiences with which the immature being interacts in the educative process.

Growth leading to more growth does not mean that an experience must be had, if it is indeed possible, free from all restraints or limitations. On the contrary, conflicts arising in the sharing of experience situations with others are essential for growth. The freedom required rests in the respect for individual traits and their full mediation with the impulses of others under the control of critical intelligence in the process of inquiry necessary to resolve the conflicts.

It is in this sense that schooling must free the conditions of experience, not in removing all barriers to impulse set by the physical and social worlds. In fact, since these limiting factors do exist, the educative process is largely a matter of meeting the resultant difficulties. Schooling, then, though it is to purify this process, is so far from negating it, that problem solving must be the medium for learning. Schooling, although distinct from the wider process of education, is expressly for the purpose of making this process and its outcomes more desirable. Therefore, the difficulties and problems which are subjects of inquiry in the school must be not only integrally related with each other and the learning child's interests for the sake of desired continuity; they must also relate directly to the same basic difficulties and problems that arise in the wider experiences of men.

We have previously had occasion to note that, for Dewey, schools should be organized as a form of community life centering in method and content about the typical occupations of men. We, perhaps, can now better appreciate the significance of the statement. For schooling must be what education would be in a society with an integrated culture where all of the institutions of society were freely participated in by all men and served the full development of all human personalities. In other words, schooling must be what education would be in a truly democratic society.

It follows that schooling must proceed in a social setting; this setting is not supplied by individuals pursuing independent ends in mere physical proximity with others; it must be a setting, as with any group we call a society, in which the members engage basically in common enterprises, no matter what variations are introduced. And, if it is to be a democratic social situation, it must be one in which all members share in making decisions that affect them. Now, to share in common enterprises, and yet not do injustice to individual traits, there must be some basic pattern of interests with which these idiosyncratic traits can be related. For integrated personalities in harmony with the social situation can be built only as the specific functions of individuals are expressed in full and free relations with their surroundings. Children are interested in the social scene about them, in the purposes and concerns of the adult world into which they are being inducted. Since the ends and values of this world have accrued to the dominant concerns of men—their occupations—then the typical occupations provide the pattern of common interests and the anchor for special interests of the members of the school community.

Harmony of these interests is not a mere state but a process. Ethical character is built through the effort to realize ideas developing from the impulses of the child within his surroundings. If the typical occupations form the core of his surroundings, they also furnish the medium for the development of impulse through desire to purpose, leading on to all the mediating agencies by which men have created and fulfilled their ends and purposes to the advantage of their impulses. Thus the method and content of schooling cannot be separated; they must be one.

This, then, is the fundamental and skeletal theory of schooling as it emerges from the foundational disciplines. The theory in its details can best be seen in operation as it functions as a guide in building a program of schooling in the Laboratory School. In the following chapter the theory will be further examined in its operational meanings.

VIII

THE LABORATORY SCHOOL

DEWEY WAS HEAD of the combined departments of Philosophy, Psychology, and Pedagogy at the University of Chicago when he started his experimental school. The latter was opened in January, 1896, with sixteen pupils and two teachers; prior to its closing in the spring of 1904, it had reached a maximum growth of one hundred and forty children from four to fifteen years of age, a regular teaching staff of twenty-three, and ten part-time assistants.[1] During its short span of existence, the school occupied three different buildings; its final home was a large frame residence with its attic and attached barn pressed into service. Although the school received much assistance in the form of cooperation from the faculty and students of the University, its financial support came principally from tuition and the generosity of parents and friends. There were three, perhaps four, stages in its career: a six-month trial-and-error period, indicative of what not to do, a two-year period of growing experiences with novel procedures, and a more settled era of steady development and refinement of practices. A fourth period, the last year of the school, 1903–4, undoubtedly was one of uncertainty and insecurity because of the pending merger with the Chicago University School of Education.

The keynote of the school's organization was flexibility. All matters pertaining to the teaching staff, equipment, space, and time were attended with reference to the principles or working hypotheses of the theory, rather than in accord with a fixed program and schedule. However, this does not mean that there was a haphazard arrangement of these factors. There was

structure in organization, its flexibility assured in the way it was conceived and administered. There was a general supervisor and a principal; there were directors, qualified by social and technical training, to head each of the several departments into which the work of the school was divided. These departments were the kindergarten, history, science and mathematics, domestic science and industries, manual training, art, music, the languages, and physical culture.

The last quarters of the school included special rooms for particular activities. There were a gymnasium, manual training rooms, art and textile studios, two science laboratories, several rooms shared by the History and English departments, and Domestic Science had a large kitchen and two dining rooms properly equipped for serving.

The pupils were not placed in grades contingent on age or the passing of the previous grade. Instead, they were grouped according to interests and abilities particularly of a social nature, which, however, corresponded roughly to chronological age. There were ultimately ten groups ranging from the kindergarten with children of four years, on up to fourteen- and fifteen-year-olds in the tenth group. Flexibility in organization, though, permitted numerous occasions for associations of all the groups in a common enterprise, plus opportunities for the older children to assume responsibility for the younger.

Time allotments for the various phases of school life were made carefully through experiment. Younger children spent from two and a half to three morning hours in the school; older ones returned for an hour and a half in the afternoon. Division of time was made, not on the basis of traditional subject-matter, but in relation to the primary focus of activity, whether dominantly handwork or intellectual work, and whether of the constructive type such as that of shop, cooking, and sewing, or of such modes of expression as modeling, painting, etc. There was developed a daily program of classes, varying from one half-hour to an hour and a half in duration.

This variability was guided by the child's level of ability and interest; it was never permitted to solidify into a rigid schedule to which the child was forced to adjust.

THE SCHOOL IN OPERATION

With this brief picture of the school as a setting, we, perhaps, are ready to examine the process of schooling as the theory became translated into actual practice. It is probable that an adequate account of this application cannot be had, short of resort to all that has been written to describe the Dewey School in operation. But our purpose may be most fruitfully served if this literature is searched for evidence of the concrete manner in which at least five aspects of the superstructure of schooling were built upon the basic framework provided by the theory. These five features will first be indicated, following which the actual practice in building each feature will be examined, with particular reference to the work of the teacher.

1. We know that the school was to be organized as a democratic social community. In any functioning community, including a democratic one, there must be leadership. The task, then, is to see how this requirement of leadership functioned in the Dewey School.

2. As the school society, rather than being isolated from the wider adult society, was expressly for the purpose of leading out into harmony with the latter, the teachers must be the representatives of adult culture. We need to know how the teachers brought adult ends and values to bear in the life of the school.

3. Perhaps to the point of annoying repetition, we have noted that these adult ends and values must be harmonized with individual traits. It is necessary to observe how the teachers sought to guide the expression of individual traits toward this required harmony.

4. In any society there must be some means of control, else the culture disintegrates. We must know what practical measures were taken to secure a disciplined community.

5. Finally, it is clear that if the teachers are to be the guides in the process of growth that is harmonious with social ends and values, they must judge particular evidences of the quality of that growth. The task, then, is to determine the actual measures used by the teachers to evaluate growth.

No claim is made that these signposts are exhaustive. However, they should guide our selection of the practices in the Dewey School sufficiently well to enable us to see the operational translation of the principal aspects of the theory, as well as the nature of the test provided for the theory. One word of warning seems in order. The theory of the school is such that all of the features selected for examination are integral parts of a pattern. Therefore some quality inevitably will be lost as these aspects are viewed separately. Nevertheless, if the interrelatedness of the features are kept in mind, it seems possible and profitable to pull each one into the foreground for special focus of attention.

1. The leadership function may be traced from the immediate association of teacher and children, through the relationship of teachers with supervisors, to the contacts of the teachers with the parents and patrons of the school. In the daily work of the school it was customary for each class to begin with conversation and discussion. After a brief period for the amenities, symbolic of group solidarity, the teacher directed the discussion to the business of the day.

The results of the previous work were reviewed in a group process, and plans for further development were discussed. Each child was encouraged to contribute either out of his past experience or imagination, ways and means of meeting the problem of needs that might arise under new circumstances. These suggestions were discussed by the group, and with the aid of the teacher, the plans for the work of the day were decided upon and delegated. At the

close of the period, there was again a group meeting when the
results, if successful, were summarized, and new plans for further
work at the next period suggested.[2]

Here the teacher's leadership function is exercised to set the
stage for group discussion and to draw out the contribution
of each child's point of view. The teacher, too, contributes
his own perspective to the planning. But the teacher is not
the only leader; for his leadership was such that leaders arose
from among the children. We learn that "the children developed their own methods of distributing important priv-
ileges." [3] Through the teacher's method of encouraging participation and responsibility on the part of each child in
deciding what was to be done, a community atmosphere was
developed such that leadership arose when needed. "In cases
of unavoidable delay on the part of teachers, the classes of all
ages, even the youngest, put themselves to work under the
direction of a leader." [4]

This same sort of leadership was in evidence in the relationships among the teachers of the school. Besides Dewey as the
head of the school, leadership positions were assigned to a
general supervisor, a principal, and to department heads. But
these positions were primarily divisions of labor rather than
of authority. "One, as principal, took charge of all contacts
with parents, graduate student-teachers, and visitors, and one,
as vice-principal, continued to assume responsibility for the
curriculum." [5] Just as leadership arose among the children
as a result of free communication and the interchange of
ideas, so among the teachers the constant sharing of ideas and
suggestions provided the atmosphere wherein leadership passed
from teacher to teacher in different situations. The teachers
with more experience, and with perhaps a better grasp of the
theory, made suggestions to younger, less experienced teachers.[6] But the contribution of each teacher was sought and
respected. Opportunities for communication among teachers
were provided through free periods and flexible schedules, as

well as in informal occasions at lunch and after school. More formal were the weekly meetings with Mr. Dewey. Here Dewey, as leader, sought to get the faculty group to problemize their difficulties in relation to the theory. The teachers' typewritten reports of the achievements and failures of the week provided the basis of their discussions.

Not only the children and teachers, but parents and patrons as well, were part of the school community. The teachers assumed leadership in inviting parents in to observe and talk over the problems of the school. This led to the formation of the Parents Association of the Laboratory School. Parents led in setting up an educational committee to receive criticisms and suggestions from the parents, and to share these with the teachers and the teachers' points of view with the parents. This finally resulted in a class where Dewey and the teachers, together with the parents, discussed the theory and practice of the school. Thus guided by the theory, the teachers set in motion the exchange of ideas back and forth from children and parents and among themselves in an atmosphere where the purposes of the school community could be located and expressed. This was what today might be called parent-teacher-pupil planning of the conditions required to harmonize the life of the child with adult ends and values.

2. The leadership exercised by the teachers in locating a community of purpose was a positive leadership which contributed adult ends and values to the process of deliberation in the school. The adult purpose was to induct the growing child into a changing and expanding adult culture with the greatest possible degree of harmony. The teacher, as representative of this culture, must understand its products and its processes, and he must contribute these as his share in the community life in such a way as to promote the full and free development of the child's traits. To achieve this purpose, he must hold and use the experiences of mankind, which have been logically organized in bodies of knowledge or technique,

as means of interpretation and guidance of the expression of individual traits. As Dewey stated it, "The systematized and defined experience of the adult mind, in other words, is of value to us in interpreting the child's life as it immediately shows itself, and in passing on to guidance and direction." [7]

This "systematized and defined experience," Dewey believed, had accrued to the basic pattern of the typical occupations of man which, therefore, were used as the fundamental framework of school life. Cooking, weaving, and sewing, woodwork and metalwork, representative of the typical needs for food, clothing, and shelter, constituted this structure in actual practice. The child entered school life with a sense of concern and involvement in these pursuits from having shared them, though in a narrow and limited way, through his membership in the family. With no sharp break in his experiences, the teachers permitted and encouraged the continued exercise of his impulses toward these familiar concerns. It was here that the teachers drew upon their adult knowledge to interpret these immediate expressions. This was no easy task; it involved much experimentation. What of abiding worth would "take hold" of the child at any moment was not self-evident. The teachers asked, "What would be a good starting point?"

Again the guiding principle answered—it must be something closely related to their own life and therefore of interest to them. Experiment only could tell whether this interest lay in the manner of living, the social and political institutions, commerce, art, literature, religion, or thought. It was a serious problem to select from all the wealth of collected knowledge that which should prove of most value for the child. [8]

Interpretations were made which, one one hand, were broadly applicable to groups of children, and, on the other hand, were specific readings of the individual child's present tendencies. [9] An illustration of broad interpretation of group interest is afforded in this example of the teachers' efforts to capitalize

upon young children's social interest. It had been decided to use Greek life as a setting in which to expand this social interest outward to the methods of warfare, commerce, politics, and domestic life which had developed from Greek social activities. It was discovered that this work was too abstract, formal, and remote for the children of the group in question. The teachers learned that the social interest at this point was related to individuals as such, in their emotional lives, in their deeds and experiences. It was found that when subject-matter was turned to the lives of individual Greeks, to the biographies of the Greek heroes, then the dynamic quality, lacking in the first approach, was reinstated. With this more adequate interpretation, the children were guided from this interest on to interest in Greek group activities and less personal arrangements and events. "As the study progressed there was a gradual passage from the concern of a single hero to those of a people who desire a common end, and, therefore, act cooperatively." [10]

Similar interpretations were made of the individual child's interests and capacities. When in the midst of the joy of popping corn he asked what caused the corn to pop, he indicated readiness for simple work in science. When in drawing he became dissatisfied with his product, he was ready for guidance in technique, form, and criticism. When in making a box his curiosity extended to the wood and where it came from, he was, perhaps, ready for reading to supply his interest. Proud of some achievement, he wished to record what he had done; he was now ready for writing. When he had observed and collected various materials, such as rocks and minerals, and then indicated a desire to see what would happen if he manipulated them, he was possibly at a stage where his interests could be turned from observational to experimental science. In all of these tendencies displayed, it was not the child who typically was conscious of the next steps.

It was the teacher with his fund of adult knowledge who read the meaning of these vague stirrings in the imagination of the child.

From the starting point furnished by interpretations made in this manner, the teacher guided the growth of these interests as they related psychologically to the experiences of the child. The work in weaving, for example, started with children's interests in activity and construction. Under the teacher's guidance this interest was related to different methods of spinning and weaving in the American Colonial period. "They learned that the invention of machines had brought many improved ways of living, had changed the organization pattern of many industries and had left many industrial and social problems for later generations to solve." [11] The children did research in encyclopaedias on methods of spinning in different parts of the world. They made use of immigrant workers in Chicago as resources for firsthand information. They constructed looms, operated spinning wheels, experimented with dyes, always guided by the teachers toward the relatedness of these activities with the wider social life. "The children realized somewhat the position of the spinner and weaver, the beginnings of organization in several branches of the industry, the misunderstanding of the value of machines and the benefit of machine work to the community, the unfortunate position of the inventor, and the riots which followed any invention replacing handwork." [12]

This brief glance at the way subject-matter was used in the school at least underscores its great significance in the experiment, and we can better understand what Dewey meant when he said:

The whole world of visual nature is all too small an answer to the problem of the meaning of the child's instinct for light and form. The entire science of physics is none too much to interpret adequately to us what is involved in some simple demand of the child for explanation of some casual change that has attracted his at-

tention. The art of Rafael or Corot is none too much to enable us to value the impulses stirring in the small child when he draws and daubs.[13]

This statement implies that knowledge of adult disciplines, of the processes through which they have developed, their inter-relatedness among each other and with man's impulses and goals—all the depth and breath of human experience—must be contributed to the school community by those who represent the wider society. Dewey was aware of the tremendous accumulation of knowledge and the consequent requirement of specialization if a sufficient degree of expertness was to be achieved. His school demanded of teachers not only comprehensive scholarship but also special competences in various subject-matters. It was professionalized competence in that the teacher needed to hold and use subject-matter as a teacher and not as a scientist. Dewey stated:

As a teacher he is not concerned with adding new facts to the science he teaches, in propounding new hypotheses or in verifying them. He is concerned with the subject-matter of the science as *representing a given stage and phase of the development of experience.*[14]

Thus his school faced a twofold problem: how to benefit from the contributions of experts without the isolation of areas of expertness that prevented harmony and integration and how to translate expertness as held by scientists into professionalized competence held by teachers.

There were two practices in the Dewey School designed to meet this problem. In order to get the benefit of expertness, the school was departmentalized with recognized heads of the various divisions. This system provided the leadership of experts in each of the areas. The clue to the solution of the difficulty arising from the tendency of departmentalization to result in compartmentalization is found in these words of Dewey's: "It is the absence of cooperative intellectual relations among the teachers that causes the present belief that young children must be taught everything by one teacher, and that leads to so-called departmental teaching being strictly compartmental with older ones." [15] Hence, it was the democratic atmosphere, the intellectual communication among the teachers, their spirit of continual investigation and experimentation, which provided both the integration of expertness and of the special competences of teachers. Better still, it was these conditions, guided by the underlying theory of the school, as we are reminded here:

When the different studies and occupations are controlled by reference to the same general principles, unity of aim and method are secured. The results obtained justify the belief that the undue separation, which often follows teaching by specialists, is a result of lack of supervision, cooperation, and control by a unified plan.[16]

The second practice used to meet the problem stemmed from the realization of limitation of teachers' expertness even when enriched by the pooling and interchange of the individual competences of the entire teaching group. Therefore, the school made use of resources in the community outside the school itself. Human resources were utilized, from the immigrants who as we have previously seen were used for their fund of information about weaving, to University of Chicago professors as specialists in their various fields. Excursions to parks, farms, and factories, to libraries and museums, were used to strengthen and vitalize the depth and range of expertness held by the faculty.

Such were the practices of the teachers in the Dewey School as they functioned as representatives of adult ends and values which they contributed to the building of the school community.

3. It must be borne in mind that the way the teachers made the contribution considered above cannot be separated from the practices adopted to help the child realize his individual traits; but we can profitably focus upon the matter of serving

the latter element of the educative process. The theory, as we know, accounted for the child as a creature of impulse, always acting toward some object or content. The expression of impulses from the very beginning of his preschool life in the family was mediated with the concerns, the procedures, and the purposes of the family. This mediation within the family led to recurrent expressions of impulse within quite similar and growingly familiar situations. By school age, these expressions had developed into four recognizable tendencies which Dewey named as interest in conversation or communication, in inquiry or finding out things, in making things or construction, and in artistic expression. He said of these fourfold interests: "We may say they are the natural resources, the uninvested capital, upon the exercise of which depends the active growth of the child." [17]

The theory made two requirements as to the use of these "natural resources": the exercise of the "uninvested capital" must take place in continuous, related situations and must lead on to the accumulation of capital gains in desire and purpose expressed in ever widening situations. In serving the first requirement, beginners in the Dewey School, four-year-old children, engaged in the familiar occupations of the home with abundant opportunity for the continued expression of impulse in the fourfold manner now grown habitual, or "instinctive." Conversation and communication among the four-year-olds was encouraged; children told of their experiences at home, of visits they had made, of what they had seen and done. "The repeated emphasis on home experiences loosened tongues, and the outside world came creeping in." [18] The daily home occupations of sewing, cooking, cleaning, washing dishes, and repair work were the centers of interest. The children dramatized many of these activities; the daily luncheon served as one medium for their social and constructive impulses as they prepared, served, and cleaned. The work was begun in a spirit of free play with the child interested in the activity for its own sake and not in attempting to discriminate means and ends. This was a period of careful interpretation on the part of the teachers who sought for signs indicating that the children were ready to expand their interests and suggestive of new and different situations which would be continuous with the old as well as serving to liberate impulses for further development.

The teachers in this school strove to meet the second requirement—that of guiding impulses through desire to purpose, fulfillment of which was to be achieved in ever expanding situations—by helping the child enlarge the scope of succeeding activities which were being woven in a continuous pattern. The free play in typical household occupations brought attention to the family's dependence on the daily visits of milkman, grocer, postman, etc. Interest in the postman, as an example, led to inquiry about his uniform, his transportation, and the letters and packages he carried. Concern with the last led on to the post office and thus outward into the wider world of human relationships. Or, again, interest in the activity of cooking was skillfully directed toward the use of number and measure for better results; on to science, as heat was seen as a form of energy to transform matter; on to the sources of food and means of production and human relations in production; or on to rituals, ceremonies, and art expressing the significance of these activities.

There were two principal techniques used by the teachers to secure this expansion of vision and purpose. The first was the free intercommunication within the group. The contribution of each child in the sharing of experiences and information served to build a group interest greater than that of any given child.

In this school, which was in character a continuation of the home, each recitation was preeminently a social meeting place where organized spontaneous conversation went on along different lines. It was the social clearing-house in which experiences and ideas

were interchanged and subjected to criticism, where misconceptions were corrected and new lines of thought and inquiry were set up.[19]

The second technique was the teachers' use of suggestion.[20] Illustrations from the work with older children may well serve to describe the use of this skill. A major project in the school was the building by the students of a clubhouse which constituted a point of departure leading out into studies in architecture, building, physiography, geometry, interior decoration, and so on. For example, in the matter of interior decoration, the children were permitted to make the mistake of choosing a stain for the walls of the clubhouse too dark for the size of the room. When the teachers suggested that the error, which had disappointed the children, might be rectified by the use of colorful curtains and cushions, the children seized the idea as an opportunity to further their purpose. They eagerly went to work with the art and textile teachers on various phases of the problem of interior decoration, far beyond that which was necessary for their immediate concern. Thus, through suggestion, impulse and eager desire were developed toward steady purpose, informed and directed by the best of relevant adult experiences.

The younger children in the school, as we have seen, engaged in familiar activities growing out of home life; through the methods and techniques used, their interests were guided outward in space and backward in time. In the beginning, these interests and activities were wholes, in the sense that means and ends were practically one. When, for example, their attention extended back to some ancient people, what held them was their social interest in persons, in the totality of their joys and sorrows, successes and failures. Only gradually did their interests become discriminatory, differentiated, and specialized. The alert teacher noted the dawning of such concerns and seized the opportunity for development along these lines. When a child in measuring material for some construction work showed curiosity about number relations, attention was given to formal mathematics and even drill work was provided. Or when another, eager to tell the content of his experiences, had difficulty with his oral or written expression, he welcomed assistance in form and technique. We are told:

On the whole the more direct modes of activity, the construction and occupational work, the scientific observation and experimentation, presented plenty of opportunities for the necessary use of reading, writing, spelling, and number work. These subjects, therefore, were not isolated studies, but were introduced as organic outgrowths of the child's daily experience.[21]

Furthermore, "expert direction was welcome because the children felt the need of being able consciously to correct their faults and gain in ability to express their ideas in voice and gesture."[22] The significance here rests with the fact that when the teachers in the Dewey School had succeeded in guiding the child's growth so that he could form and purpose ends requiring skill and precision in means, then they gave direct and conscious attention to improvement of means, and, it should be added, without losing sight of the end. Thus the interest which served as a starting point was sustained, not by focusing upon any activity having only immediate interest for the child, but through guidance toward the awareness of relationships between what was purposed and the necessary steps in the achievement of the goal.

Up to this point we have been concerned with the overt development of the child's traits, but as Dewey reminds us, "the real child, it hardly need be said, lives in the world of imaginative values and ideas which find only imperfect outward embodiment."[23] The imagination, for Dewey, was no special part of the child, but the medium in which he lives. This was the medium recognized in the school for much of the development of expression, of inquiry, and of creativity. The teachers helped to vitalize this imagination through the dramatic interchange of ideas in recitations. They led the

children to dramatize real-life scenes of people remote in time and space, where the children in different roles relived in imagination stirring and meaningful events and situations. They provided opportunity and encouragement for creative expression in all art mediums, not excluding those often considered industrial and meanly practical.

The ideal of the school was that the music, the literary and dramatic efforts of the children, and their artistic expression whether in design, in wood, metal or fabric, in the graphic or plastic arts—all should represent the culmination, the idealization, the highest point of refinement of all the work carried on.[24]

The teacher guided the growth of the imagination to these culminating creative expressions of individual traits out of the matrix of interest and concern with the basic occupational activities of men and through the mediating influences of adult ends and values. Thus was individuality to be anchored in social realities and harmonized with social values. In this way the teachers sought to realize Dewey's hope:

Where we now see only the outward doing and the outward product, there, behind all visible results, is the readjustment of mental attitude, the enlarged and sympathetic vision, the sense of growing power, and the willing ability to identify both insight and capacity with the interests of the world and of men.[25]

4. In any society there must be order and control; otherwise, aimless and random activity prevails and anarchy and chaos result. So, in the Dewey School, there was order and control. We have previously noted the orderly division of responsibility among the members of the faculty. Similar orderliness obtained in the curriculum; there were time schedules, the distribution of rooms and equipment, the division of the curriculum into focal, though not isolated, courses. But this order was neither in theory nor in fact a rigid system of set behavior patterns. It was, instead, a flexible order, flexible in that schedules, rooms, equipment, and courses were readily altered

to further the work of the school, but yet an order in that changes or revisions of previous plans were guided by the underlying theory. It was the experimental approach, with ideas and plans arising in the spirit of inquiry, which achieved flexibility combined with orderliness.

But it was not so much in the mechanics of school organization or administration that control was sought or attained. Rather it was expected and achieved within the process of living in the school community, within a process guided by social intelligence. Control stemmed from the daily, even hourly, interchange of ideas among teachers and pupils, where purposes were formed and plans made to execute them. The teachers, as leaders in this process, curbed any tendency the pupils may have had to accept too hastily inadequately formed purposes and plans by insisting that they be weighed, through reflection, against previous experiences, and with consideration for possible consequences.

The teacher's part was to answer questions and by skilfull refreshing of the children's memories to insure that plans for the day were workable and also different enough in character to furnish a new experience involving a problem for the group.[26]

With the problem formulated, control was sustained by the teacher's emphasis on what the school called the "test and see" attitude. Thus it was adherence to intelligent group deliberation and the experimental method which controlled the life of the school.

The maintenance of discipline and control, then, was a function of the teacher only as leader in the development of democratic, intelligent control among the members of the school community. With younger children, this leadership responsibility extended to many areas of little conscious concern to children of this age. But with growing ability on the part of the children to relate means to more remote ends, responsibility was sought by the children and relinquished to

them. The teachers used the problem approach in an atmosphere of community concern to get this desired development of a sense of responsibility for the quality of work performed as it affected the welfare of the group. As the children engaged in activities directed toward their goals they were led to see that desirable acts were those most fully interrelated with the acts and goals of others. Hence, this principle was the criterion and ideal which caused responsible discipline to become a function of each individual in the school community.

With the basic framework of the life of the school centered in the typical occupations of men, the difficulties encountered in these activities were the elements which were problemized, so that there was usually common interest and concern in the solutions achieved. But, again as in any society, there were individuals whose special interests and traits deviated from the common, and who found it difficult to relate their concerns with those of others—individuals who endangered the common control. Witness the following situation and the way it was handled. One of the older groups was using an historical approach to the study of what, fundamentally, was geological science.

There were in this group, however, and in several of the older groups a number of boys who were irked by the historical approach and who seemed to require a shift in method. Their interests were not in line with those of the rest of the children; their attention was divided or entirely lacking; and their efforts in accord with their interest, either retarded or interfered with those of the others. These boys were finally taken out of the class and allowed to follow their own devices and individual lines until the general trend of their interests could be determined.[27]

The teachers saw that loss of control was really loss of continuity and indentification with the group enterprise. Their technique was to supply conditions of permissive and free expression while they could interpret the traits being exercised, and on the basis of their adult knowledge, seize the point of contact and from this guide the boys toward the re-establishment of continuity with group purposes.[28]

Control, then, was sought within the democratic process of community living, where those concerned shared in planning their activities, subject to the best possible use of group intelligence, and subject also to leadership in the maintenance of group responsibility. Thus both freedom and control developed with the child's growing ability to share in making intelligent and responsible choices.

5. The teachers in the Dewey School were, according to the theory, to act as guides in the process of the growth of students toward harmony of individual traits with social ends and values. As leaders in the school community, it was necessary that they should engage in a continuous process of judging the quality of that growth. In accord with the theory, the best assurance that growth was occurring came from evidence that each was mediating his impulses fully within the developing situations of the school community. And, since this harmony of function and situation is both the ideal and the criterion of the moral act, then the achievement of such unity of experience was judged desirable, as well as successful.

It is possible to distinguish at least four interrelated types of evidence used by the teachers in the Dewey School to evaluate integrated growth. In the first place, there were signs indicative of increased ability to relate means and ends. For the beginning child, the expression of impulse tended to be both the manner and goal of the exercise of his functions, and was thus play. Out of the continuity of his experiences there came moments when he hesitated, when he delayed immediate action toward his dominant desire in order to plan and execute satisfactory means of achieving his goal. Such occasions were taken by the teachers as a sign of growth. This evaluative principle was expressed this way:

As the child grows in experience, he is able to see an act, a thing, or an idea, not by itself, but as part of a larger, perhaps coveted

whole. This act may be a means of gaining the larger whole, and his interest expands to using this means to attain this end. He meets difficulty in using these means; this stimulates him to think more clearly and intensely of what it is he wants, and what he must do to get it. His end becomes not alone an object of desire; it is something worth working for. Interest, therefore, steadies and enlists effort and stimulates thoughtful action. Increasing willingness to delay action, to perfect means in order to arrive at larger ends, is indicative of increasing maturity.[29]

Typical of the way this willingness showed itself in maturing ability, as the teachers interpreted it, is this illustration:

Children of eight years, at the end of a long course in experimental cooking, were able to make a general classification of foods, grouping those together which required the same or similar means of preparation by cooking. At eleven years, when their experience had included experiments in solution and osmosis, and a physiological study of animals, these same children reclassified foods on the basis of their use to the body.[30]

A second type of evidence, following from the first, was found in the results of this willingness and ability to plan means to achieve ends, for the test of these attitudes and powers was the way they passed over into action. The whole spirit of the school, as we know, was active, not passive. Plans were not only made, they were acted upon. Since the planning was a cooperative community enterprise, each individual's share in the execution of the plans was judged, not by how he fared in competition with the others, but by the value of his contribution in furthering the common enterprise. Thus each was evaluated by a comparison of his abilities with the quality of his production, and this evaluation was shared by pupils as well as teachers in the interchange of ideas and suggestions concerning the successes and failures in the execution of their plans. The significance of this standard for judgment is shown in Dewey's statement:

So far as emulation enters in, it is the comparison of individuals, not with regard to the quantity of information personally absorbed, but with reference to the quality of work done—the genuine community standard of value.[31]

Extending further this concept of a community standard of value, we recognize a third criterion of evaluation. The quality of work was not judged in isolation, as merely the child's own, but also for its social import. The responsibility shown in doing his best, not for himself alone, but for the welfare of the group, was taken by the teachers as a sign of harmonious development. This was, in no sense, a negation or restriction of his own self-interest. As the teachers saw it:

Each individual, however, has a different make-up and endowment, a unique point of view which places him in a unique relationship to the social process of the group. He, therefore, reflects the social attitudes and relations uniquely. In the process of interaction each child gradually becomes conscious of himself as a self that is a factor in these relations. He thus realizes others and himself in a social situation in which they and he both take part. Growth, therefore, depends upon reciprocal relationships in a suitable environment.[32]

The teachers carefully observed the child's activities and attitudes which indicated his adjustment to these reciprocal relationships and they evaluated his growth by the quality of adjustment shown. "The conscious direction of his actions toward considered social ends became an unfailing index of the child's progress toward maturity." [33]

The fourth criterion used by the teachers to evaluate the process of harmonious growth was the emotional accompaniment of development, which they described as happiness. The teachers believed that "the emotional accompaniment of such progressive growth of activity, of continual movement, of expansion, and of achievement is happiness." The signs indicative of this happiness were, in no sense, necessarily expressions of

spontaneous joyousness, or other familiarly accepted outward tokens of pleasure. Instead, the teachers read happiness in the absorbed interest, in the identification of self and on-going activity fundamentally social in nature.

Judgment as to whether there was a right learning condition in the classroom was often based on the attitude (poised and happy, or nervous and irritable) of the child as he went to the next class. A quiet and contented attitude was considered an indication of satisfaction of desire arising from the successful accomplishment of a planned end. Such an attitude also indicated that the teacher was fulfilling her fuction.[34]

The teachers operated on the principle that this absorbed interest and identification of self with what one was about was an indication of growth and was happiness. "Persons, whether children or adults, are interested in what they do successfully. They have a sense of confidence and accomplishment. This absorbed interest means a happiness which is not self-consciousness and is a sign of developing power." [35] With happiness thus taken as the sustaining emotional concomitant of continuous and expanding experiences, the teacher judged the happy child to be the growing child.

· IX ·

AN ASSESSMENT OF
DEWEY'S THEORY OF SCHOOLING

THE NEED for a more adequate theory and practice of schooling, in Dewey's view, had become an urgent requirement in the closing years of the nineteenth century. For the purpose of schooling was to help solve the increasingly urgent problem of education—the harmonizing of individual traits with social ends and values. Schooling, as a conscious and deliberate effort to attend to this problem, was required because of the increasing strength of the barriers to the achievement of harmony through the informal educative processes of the wider society. The mounting difficulties stemmed from social conditions which were creating wider and wider gaps in and among the experiences of men.

Hence, for the theory and practice of schooling to be adequate for its task, it must meet two sets of several requirements. First, it must be based upon a diagnosis of social conditions which reflects a sound and complete interpretation of the current situation. Secondly, it must be consistent with interrelated theories of human experience and its various aspects of behavior, thought, judgment, and relationships—with theories of psychology, logic, ethics, and social philosophy—which themselves consistently reveal the possibilities for the solution of the problem and offer support and guidance to the effort. Any evaluation of Dewey's theory of schooling, then, must consider its adequacy with respect to both of these requirements.

THE CONSISTENCY OF THE THEORY OF SCHOOLING
WITH THE FOUNDATIONAL DISCIPLINES

Turning first to the second requirement—the consistency of the theory with the foundational disciplines—we find that this criterion has, in effect, already been applied. In Chapter VII, Dewey's views of psychology, logic, ethics, and social philosophy were focally seen as contributions to the solution of the problem of education as Dewey defined it. They were seen as supports to the theory of schooling which Dewey shaped as an experimental solution to the problem. The result of the attempt showed the marked consistency of Dewey's major views of psychology, logic, ethics, and social philosophy with his theory of schooling which was developing currently. Their relationship was such that one might derive the principles of the educational theory from the principles enunciated in the foundational disciplines. Moreover, the consideration of these disciplines with the problem of education in mind showed even a closer inner consistency. The foundational disciplines themselves are interwoven in a pattern which sustains the view that the unity and harmony of the experiences in the life of an individual and the life of a society are theoretically both possible and desirable. In no sense, for example, does the function of thought in experience deny or oppose the function of impulse; neither does the ethical ideal transcend and set itself off from thought or desire; nor does the view of social relationships isolate the experiences of any individual from those of his fellows. The gaps within experience in the 1890's were, on this view, practical and institutional, not theoretical. The foundational disciplines were thus designed to give theoretical guidance to the task of sustaining and guiding schooling as an agency for overcoming those practical and institutional barriers to an harmonious and unified common experience.

To say that the disciplines are thus consistent with the theory of schooling is, perhaps, warrantable. But this does not mean, of necessity, that the integration of the foundational disciplines with the theory of schooling is complete, or that Dewey had developed all of the foundational disciplines which are conceivably relevant to a theory of schooling. In the first place, it would be too much to claim that every aspect of Dewey's broader theorizing found its way into his theory of schooling. For example, we may recall that at one point in the development of his thinking, Dewey hinted that there might be some sex differences in the function of thought. In denying any native conservative intelligence in women as contrasted with radical intelligence in men on the grounds that the notion stemmed from social conditions, he did say that female intelligence might be radical as to means, male intelligence radical as to ends. This suggests that the specific functions of individuals might include special functions in women which men could not fully share. Conversely, there might be special male functions in which women could not completely participate. Dewey did not pursue this distinction into his theory of schooling or, so far as we know, into the program of the school. However, it is probably fair to say that it would not have involved any major break with the rest of his theoretical structure. For though such special functions were not shared directly or intimately, their meaning and significance could be, and thus remain consistent with collaboration of the sexes in the community of the school. But while attention to this aspect would have made no major difference in his theory of schooling, it might have suggested special opportunities in the school program for the exercise of specialized functions and distinctive occupations characteristic of each sex.

With respect to any inadequacy of scope in the foundations, the neglect of explicit reference to the religious aspects of experience may be pointed out. Dewey's later treatment of the philosophy of religion suggests the high degree of consistency

between his interpretation of religion and the notion of the complete ethical act expressed in the theory of the 1890's.[1] While this omission in his thought at the time of the experimental school may be regretted, it seems probable that, in light of later developments of his thought, its inclusion would not have detracted from but rather have added to the integration of his foundational theory.

This same point applies to any neglect of an explicit theory of aesthetics in the 1890's, an omission suggested by Harold Rugg.[2] Again, when later Dewey expressed systematically his views on this aspect of experience, he merely made explicit what was to a large extent implied in the foundational theories already formulated at the time when his school was organized.[3]

While it may be possible to denote other evidences of incompleteness, the striking fact which stands out in all of our examination of Dewey's theory is its high degree of internal consistency. Further, the theoretical basis of schooling supplied by Dewey is so complete that it contrasts sharply with many of the current notions of schooling which were based upon one-sided foundational emphases, whether psychological, ethical, or logical. The educational movements previously surveyed in Chapter VI are cases in point. There are, then, good grounds for claiming a high degree of consistency and integrity between Dewey's theory of schooling and his treatment of the foundational disciplines.

THE ADEQUACY OF DEWEY'S SOCIAL DIAGNOSIS

If schooling is necessary to meet the problem of education which has become critical because of social conditions, then it must be based upon a full and accurate diagnosis of the social situation. This is the other requirement which Dewey's theory of schooling must meet consistently and adequately. Here again, it seems that our examination of his view of the social situation and the theory of schooling devised to counter these conditions as an aid to the educative process shows the consistency attained through keeping the problem near the focus of his inquiry. But to say that there was great consistency is not to say that his social diagnosis and prescription for schooling were unqualifiedly adequate. But, once more, this statement does not imply any extreme inadequacy; rather, it suggests that a more complete diagnosis might have led to somewhat different emphases in the prescription and its application.

Dewey's social analysis, as we have seen, centered about the tremendous effects of science and technology in the creation and accentuation of the divisions in and among the experiences of men. Though he insisted upon the critical nature of the resultant conflicts, still he may have underestimated their full effect on the social life of the time. He possibly assumed that children entered school with impulses and modes of expression which, though quite circumscribed by the narrow life of the home, were relatively common to all. By his own theory, if the situations in which a child exercised his functions differed greatly from those of others, his interests, his modes of expression, also would vary in the same degree. Dewey, perhaps, carried in his head a picture of a typical family situation common in the first years of life; yet the same extremes of wealth, social position, and ethical standing of the breadwinner's occupation, to which he had pointed, suggests that his picture may have been far from typical.

Dewey's theory of schooling, as we know, anticipated differences in experiences and called for the sharing of these experiences through communication and discussion. It was assumed that these interchanges would center in the common interests stemming from family life. But the question is whether the divisive influences of social life had gone so far as to stunt or divert the interests of at least some children to the extent that they bore only remote relationships to the dominant interests typical of other children and other parts of

adult society. In the degree that this was the case, the theory and practice of schooling would need to concentrate on building common needs and interests and assume less ready-made mutual concerns as a starting point. The theory would need to serve as a guide to the teachers as they led the search for a community of purpose when, perhaps, there was little community of interest which could be assumed at the beginning. To the extent that unique experiences and barriers of caste, class, and occupation create this particular difficulty, in the same degree, it would seem, schooling should be focused upon it.

It is not our purpose here to complete what may have been a partially inadequate social diagnosis, nor to add to the prescription and application necessary to deal with a heightened difficulty. But, from the factor in the prevailing social conditions which has been suggested as underemphasized, it seems to follow that schooling, as a conscious and deliberate attempt to meet the problem of education, might need to be extended to the task of bridging the gaps between the families in which children shape their original impulses. The theory of schooling, of course, provided for this extension *from* the schooling of children; it, perhaps, should have given more direct attention to this factor as a necessary support *for* the adequate schooling of children. And, it seems that schooling would need to provide for the victims of situations markedly deviant from those dominant at the moment by including the services of therapy to heal the effects upon personality of stunted and bizarre experiences.

In fairness to Dewey's diagnosis and prescription, it must be remembered that these inadequacies are suggested from the vantage point provided by an additional fifty years' experience of a divided culture. Dewey had not read the social situation as static but as dynamic and growing increasingly critical. In 1936, in writing of the problem of education he said: "The problem is especially difficult at the present time because of the conflicts in the traditions, beliefs, customs, and institutions which influence social life today." [4] Thus, by this time, he seemed less optimistic at two points than he had been in making his diagnosis of the social situation at the time of his school.

One point involves the fact and significance of social change brought about by the development of science and technology. It will be recalled that he had accepted this as a vital phenomenon obvious to all. He seemed to assume that people had a deep sense of change and were confused and uncertain regarding the relations between changed conditions and their daily lives; therefore, schooling was to help them see and understand these relationships. The confusion and uncertainty probably existed, but when he assumed that people were quite conscious of change he may have overlooked the possibility that the confusion extended both to inability to read any significance in the expanding alternatives of life and to resistance against change in traditions, beliefs, customs, and institutions, even in the midst of the changing conditions of life. This suggests that a more complete view of the social situation which included these possibilities might have led to some different emphases in the theory of schooling. It may have pointed more toward sensitizing children to change and the reconstruction of attitudes with respect to the assessment and evaluation of change and resistance to change. There is no doubt that this factor was included in Dewey's theory of schooling. But schooling, we recall, is a conscious and deliberate effort; some elements of the task are more consciously recognized and deliberately emphasized than others. The suggested interpretation of social conditions, if included in the basis of schooling, might heighten the degree of alert attention to these difficulties.

The second point of early optimism centered in Dewey's belief that, though men did not see yet that "democracy" must include the idea that all men must share in the creation of the

good life, they did at least tend to agree that all should share equitably in the products of the good life. But the material products had always been scarce, and this tended to warp the spiritual products. Perhaps the case was so much so that even though men may have had the ideal of sharing both, it was held with many reservations and with fearful comparisons with past conditions. Many men, perhaps, did not yet have a vision of the possibilities of democratic sharing even in the products of industrial life, to say nothing of lack of insight into the significance of free participation in their creation. It is possible that Dewey's own vision somewhat obscured the lack of it in others. His theory called for the school to be a democratic society. But, again, the question is whether the theory emphasized the building of a community of purpose within a situation already pervaded with the democratic vision. Perhaps it underestimated the need for focusing upon the task of clarifying and vitalizing that vision.

These suggestions of inadequacies in Dewey's social diagnosis and their limiting effect upon his theory of schooling do not indicate a fatal weakness; they do not point to a rejection of his views and the necessity of a search for an alternative theoretical foundation for schooling. Rather, they indicate some possibilities for an extension of his fruitful attempt to formulate a solution to the problem of education as he sought to define it. His own theory recognized the requirement of extension and reconstruction. He made no claims of having solved or defined the problem once and for all. It may be well to recall what he said in 1936:

The problem of the relation between individual freedom and collective well-being is today urgent and acute, perhaps more so than at any time in the past. The problem of achieving both these values without the sacrifice of either one is likely to be the dominant problem of civilization for many years to come. . . . In any case, it is an ever-renewed problem, one which each new generation has to solve over again for itself.[5]

But to "solve over again" does not imply a *de novo* solution. It may well be sought through the extension and continuing reconstruction of probably the most fruitful and democratic theory of schooling we have.[6]

THE CONGRUENCE OF THE THEORY WITH ITS APPLICATION

When we turn to an assessment of the degree of consistency found in the relationship between the operations of the Laboratory School and the theory of schooling, one consideration is the congruence of the theory with its application. It must be understood that the application was itself an experimental process. There was, admittedly, an early trial-and-error period where tentative practices were found to be inconsistent and inadequate; this stage, by description, was a negative application in the sense of pointing at what not to do. Even beyond this first period, the significant interpretive and guidance functions of the teachers were never an easy matter. Also, the fact that there was little in the way of previous experience in these functions, and few suitable materials and equipment for the required procedures, makes it safe to assume that immediate practices were not seldom out of step with the theory.

Dewey, himself, has drawn attention to this probability, suggesting three areas of difficulty in application. In the first place, the school's policies and procedures were based upon a broad and clear perspective of the nature of the individual and his psychological growth and development. But there were few data and limited experimental evidence concerning the concrete, particular details of this process. For experimental purposes, then, the school found it necessary to give undue individual freedom of action in order to discover the functions and interests of the students which were to serve as the starting point for the building of personality. In the second place, the theory required testing by teachers who were to guide community living through democratic leadership. Adults whose

own education had provided little opportunity for sharing in the control of their school experiences and whose concepts of the requirements of such a role were extremely limited had great difficulty devising the methods and techniques necessary for the test. In the third place, traditional subject-matter was identified with ready-made products of knowledge. The theory, on the other hand, called for a synthesis of product with process and the continuity of this synthesis with the child's needs and interests. With available content materials more of a hindrance than a help, much experimentation was required and, no doubt, many false leads were pursued.[7]

Two further suggestions of inadequacies are related to the composition of the student body and the limited duration of the school. The experimental application of the theory was circumscribed by the fact that the students represented a select group. For, we are told, they came for the most part from professional families.[8] This means that there was probably insufficient opportunity to interpret as great diversity of interests as might have been more typical. Consequently, experimental search for content which would connect with present social functions was possibly incomplete. The weakness in regard to the duration of the school stems from the abrupt closing of the school. At the end the first pupils had attained the age of only about fourteen. This was unintentional, but nevertheless extremely regrettable. For these pupils had developed the ability to relate means to more remote ends and were ready to pass from historic to experimental science. Some of them had, no doubt, already reached this point and there was some experimentation at this level. But the time was too short to settle into a satisfactory pattern of procedures. Another factor preventing adequate inquiry here was the necessity of taking time to drill pupils of this age for college entrance examinations. As a visitor to the school remarked, this was unfortunate and due, not to the type of schooling the children had previously received, but to the nature of the examinations.[9]

The theory had conceived the unity and continuity of schooling through the university level but the experiment in application was stopped before this was achieved.

All in all, there were many handicaps to the faithful applications of Dewey's theory of schooling in the Laboratory School. Many mistakes were made; many false leads were pursued; many techniques and procedures were devised only to be discarded as inadequate expressions of the theory. Yet, where time and resources permitted, there gradually emerged consistent practices and satisfactory procedures. It is probably too much to say that the application as a whole was highly congruent with the theory. But it can be said that there was a consistent attempt to locate adequate practices under the constant guidance of the theory. If inquiry did not disclose entirely suitable measures, at least it did not rest easy with sanctification of procedures incongruous with the theory.

THE LABORATORY SCHOOL AS A TEST OF THE THEORY

In addition to a consideration of the school as an application of the theory, there is the question of its function as a test of the theory. From the nature of Dewey's philosophy, we know that thought must be completed in action; a theory must be tested by acting upon it. Two statements made by Dewey regarding this function of the school bear so directly on the point that they are worthy of careful attention. In 1936, he referred to the objective of the school, as stated at the time of its opening, and said that by intention it was an experimental school.

Its aim was to test certain ideas which were used as working hypotheses. These ideas were derived from philosophy and psychology, some perhaps would prefer to say a philosophical interpretation of psychology. The underlying theory of knowledge emphasized the part of problems, which originated in active situations, in the development of thought and also the necessity of testing

thought by action if thought was to pass over into knowledge. The only place in which a comprehensive theory of knowledge can receive an active test is in the process of education. It was also thought that the diffused, scattering, and isolated state of school studies provided an unusual situation in which to work out in the concrete, instead of merely in the head or on paper, a theory of the unity of knowledge.[10]

Now the purpose of schooling, as we know, was to help solve the problem of education. The test of schooling devised for this task, then, would seem ultimately to be whether or not it actually rendered the assistance to the broader educative process. But in these remarks, Dewey indicates that the school was to test a theory of the unity of knowledge. This raises the question of the relationship between testing this theory and the final test of the theory of schooling required for its task. Dewey explained the intended relationship, it seems, when he wrote these words in *The School and Society*:

Now the purpose of performing an experiment is that other people need not experiment; at least need not experiment so much, may have something definite and positive to go by. An experiment demands particularly favorable conditions in order that results may be reached both freely and securely. It has to work unhampered, with all the needed resources at command. Laboratories lie back of all the great business enterprises of today, back of every great factory, every railway and steamship system. Yet the laboratory is not a business enterprise; it does not aim to secure for itself the conditions of business life, nor does the commercial undertaking repeat the laboratory. There is a difference between working out and testing a new truth, or a new method, and applying it on a wide scale, making it available for the mass of men, making it commercial. But the first thing is to discover the truth, to afford all necessary facilities, for this is the most practical thing in the world in the long run. We do not expect to have other schools literally imitate what we do. A working model is not something to be copied; it is to afford a demonstration of the feasibility of the principle, and of the methods which make it feasible. So (to come back to our own point) *we want here to work out the problem of the unity, the organization of the school system in itself, and to do this by relating it so intimately to life as to demonstrate the possibility and necessity of such organization for all education.*[11]

Here is the notion that the Laboratory School was to experiment with procedures for unifying and organizing the school system. This was to be done in such a way as to demonstrate the feasibility of the principle of the unity of knowledge. Also, it was to work out the methods which make it feasible. The unity of knowledge was central to the process of harmonious development of individual traits and social ends and values. The nature of the methods to be worked out in support of this principle can best be summed up in the term "democratic." If the school could devise democratic procedures leading to the unity of knowledge and harmony of experience, it would point to the *possibility* and *necessity* of such organization for all education, that is, for education in its wider sense of social living. If the school experiment could show that under conditions of democracy, gaps in experience, within and among individuals, could be eliminated, it would fortify the place of democracy in a desirable educative process. The wider society would not have to "experiment so much," it "would have something positive and definite to go by." With the feasibility and necessity demonstrated, it could confine its own experimentation within a democratic framework.

Therefore, the school as a test of the theory was primarily an evaluation of the procedures tried out for setting up the democratic conditions required for the growth of harmony between individual traits and social ends and values. We have already seen, in our discussion of the school as an application of the theory, that as various practices were inaugurated they were evaluated for the consistency and adequacy with which they met the conditions prescribed by the theory. The techniques for evaluating the children's growth in the unity of knowledge and experience were measures that indicated the

quality of the procedures used. Such measurement, then, was a test of the unity and organization of the school itself. In the school, the evaluation of the progress of the children served as a diagnosis for the teachers. This was to determine the worth of the methods and techniques used and to suggest hypotheses for their modification and extension in further inquiry.

As the school grew out of the problem of education in its wider sense, so its work and achievements were to pass back into the process of education. This return was expected along two paths. One was by way of demonstration of the possibility and necessity of furthering desirable education through truly democratic conditions of life. The other was through the adult activities of the children who were trained under such conditions through the conscious and deliberate effort of schooling. They were expected to continue striving for full mediation of their experiences with those of others. The lifelong quality of this mediation would be the measure of the child's education.

Dewey expected that, "when the school introduces and trains each child of society into membership within such a little community, saturating him with the spirit of service, and providing him with the instruments of effective self-direction, we shall have the deepest and best guaranty of a larger society which is worthy, lovely and harmonious." [12] It is, then, a well-ordered society, created by effective self-directed persons who realize their individualities through such creative efforts, which is to be the final test of the theory. Such a qualitative situation is predicted for the time when the conditions of the educative process are all as stated and implied in the theoretical structure formulated to guide the solution of the problem of education. If, under these essentially democratic conditions, this quality pervades the processes of individual and social life, the theory is warranted.

It is the function of the school to inquire into and evaluate the procedures for securing these conditions within its own miniature society. It would then assist the broader educative process in two ways: first, by demonstrating the feasibility and necessity for democratic conditions for this process and, second, by guiding the growth of character in youth which will sustain these conditions in life. That the Laboratory School successfully achieved the second assistance to education can neither be affirmed nor denied, since no adequate measure exists.[13] But the testimony of the members of the small society given thirty years after the school closed offers little ground for denial.[14] Similarly inconclusive is the school's demonstration of the first way it sought to aid education. At least it seems fair to state that the results of this experiment have not fully "passed back into the common sense" out of which the experiment arose. Yet the comprehensiveness and vitality of Dewey's ideas are such that they persist in making the return. Though his ideas, as stated at the outset, are often misinterpreted and misapplied, even in the face of this circumstance, it is probable that it is his inquiry, his experiment, which has most forcefully induced and sustained the continuing struggle toward democratic conditions for schooling.

But there is one sense, at least, in which the school as a test of the theory seems quite conclusive. For it tested also what Dewey saw as the requirements for educational theory, whether for his own or for alternative theories designed by others. When these requirements are met the result is not absolute perfection, but it is, basically, a conceptual structure which enables teachers "to know what they are about." And "to know what they are about" means to know what specific ideas in the theory are working and which are falling down. The teachers putting the ideas of Dewey's theoretical structure into operation did not have the perfect answer to all possible difficulties; what they did have was a key to locating what was wrong with their answers. Because Dewey met his requirements for educational theory, the teachers in his school suffered no basic contradictions or confusions. When any im-

mediate procedure went awry or did not achieve the results predicted, or when any one practice seemed to undo the results of another—in such situations the teachers had as their guide toward better practices a system of ideas unusually adequate in scope and consistency. The teachers had a problem to solve; they had a multifaceted goal and well-defined obstacles to overcome for its attainment. They had an hypothesis of equally great dimensions for the solution of the problem; that is, they had consistently interrelated conceptions of the basic human disciplines to sustain them in holding to the possibility of its solution and to guide them in their test of the hypothesis. The record of the Dewey School shows no one-sided emphasis on practices derived on one hand almost exclusively from psychology, or on the other from an ethics with no supporting psychology. There was no one-sided focus on the individual which disregarded the social conditions for individuality, nor a social focus that violated human personality. There was no imbalance of the products or processes of inquiry such that the subject-matter was separated from method, or that the processes went on in the proverbial vacuum. To illustrate the point more specifically, there were no confusions such as in the case where the attempt is made to combine intuitive and hedonistic theories.[15]

There is no intention here of claiming that the situation is such with respect to Dewey's theories that any alternatives proposed are inherently in error. It goes without saying that it is possible to object to, or even to reject, aspects of Dewey's thought in psychology, logic, ethics, or social philosophy. It is possible to question his formulation of the problem of education and his social diagnosis with both the potentialities and the barriers he saw in it. What is intended, however, is the claim that Dewey set necessarily comprehensive demands for educational theory and faithfully met them with unusual thoroughness. This is so much the case that his plea for others to participate in reconstructing his ideas was no mere exhortation. For his own theories made this reconstruction both possible and fruitful because they serve as intelligent guides even toward their own omissions and errors. Thus the thoroughness of his conceptual structure was such that, rather than being constrained within its own system, it extended even to the provision of a springboard toward its own further development. Serious and intelligent students and critics of Dewey's ideas will add to the stature of their own ideas and criticisms, and to the improvement of current educational procedures and products, to the extent that their educational theorizing meets similarly rigorous requirements equally well. When it does, swifter progress is predicted toward such schooling of the child as will provide "the deepest and best guaranty of a larger society which is worthy, lovely, and harmonious."

NOTES

I: INTRODUCTION

1. Robert Ulich, *History of Educational Thought*, New York: American Book Co., 1945, p. 333.

2. John Childs, *Education and Morals*, New York: Appleton-Century-Crofts, Inc., 1950, p. 152.

3. Ulich says of Dewey that, "had he from the beginning expressed himself so unambiguously about the necessity of regulative and persistent values as he did after 1930 . . . the line from Franklin, Pestalozzi, and Froebel to Emerson, and from Emerson to Francis Parker and Dewey himself, would have been much more evident." (Ulich, *History of Educational Thought*, p. 335.)

Yet Professor Butts says, "While paying his respects to Pestalozzi, Froebel, and Herbart, Dewey drew principally upon the growing forces of democracy, science, industrialism, evolution, and pragmatism for support." (R. Freeman Butts, *A Cultural History of Education*, New York: McGraw-Hill Book Co., 1947, p. 525.)

These passages illustrate both the uncertainty of the lines of influence and the conflicting interpretations of Dewey's ideas.

4. John T. Wahlquist, *Philosophy of American Education*, New York: The Ronald Press Co., 1942, p. 175.

5. *Ibid.*, p. 91.

6. Newton Edwards and Herman Richey, *The School in the American Social Order*, Boston: Houghton Mifflin Co., 1947, p. 734.

7. Wahlquist, *Philosophy of American Education*, p. 101.

8. Katherine Camp Mayhew and Anna Camp Edwards, *The Dewey School*, New York: D. Appleton-Century Co., 1936, p. 464. Quotations reproduced by permission of Appleton-Century-Crofts, Inc.

9. Morton G. White, *The Origin of Dewey's Instrumentalism*, New York: Columbia University Press, 1943.

10. M. H. Thomas and H. W. Schneider, *A Bibliography of John Dewey*, New York: Columbia University Press, 1929, p. xii.

11. See Harold Rugg, *Foundations for American Education*, New York: World Book Co., 1947.

II: PSYCHOLOGY

1. Morton G. White, *The Origin of Dewey's Instrumentalism*, New York: Columbia University Press, 1943, p. 9.

2. John Brubacher, *A History of the Problems of Education*, New York: McGraw-Hill Book Co., Inc., 1947, p. 148.

3. John Dewey, *Leibniz's New Essays Concerning the Human Understanding*, Chicago: S. C. Grigg and Co., 1888, p. 272.

4. John Dewey, *Psychology*, New York: Harper and Brothers, 1887, p. 6.

5. John Dewey, "The Psychological Standpoint," *Mind*, XI (1886), 19.

6. Dewey, *Leibniz's New Essays*, p. 62.

7. White, *The Origin of Dewey's Instrumentalism*, p. 62.

8. John Dewey, "Review of *Elementary Psychology* by J. H. Baker," *Educational Review*, i (May, 1891), 496.

9. White, *The Origin of Dewey's Instrumentalism*, p. 121.

10. William James, "Are We Automata?" *Mind*, IV (1879), 12.

11. *Ibid.*, p. 11.

12. John Dewey, "Social Psychology," *Psychological Review*, I (July, 1894), 400–411.

13. *Ibid.*, p. 403.   14. *Ibid.*   15. *Ibid.*, p. 404.

16. *Ibid.*, p. 408.   17. *Ibid.*

18. John Dewey, "The Reflex Arc Concept," *Psychological Review*, III (July, 1896), 357–70.

19. *Ibid.*, p. 370.

20. John Dewey, "The Theory of Emotion. I. Emotional Attitudes," *Psychological Review*, I (Nov., 1894), 553–69.

21. John Dewey, "The Theory of Emotion. II. The Significance of Emotions," *Psychological Review*, II (Jan., 1895), 13–32.

22. *Ibid.*, p. 18.   23. *Ibid.*, p. 22.   24. *Ibid.*, p. 31.

25. John Dewey, "Interest in Relation to Training of the Will," in *National Herbart Society, Second Supplement to the Herbart Yearbook for 1895*, Bloomington, Ill., 1896.

26. Dewey says in his intellectual autobiography that only when his thinking was schematic was writing easy. White believes it was when Dewey turned from Idealism to Instrumentalism that his

writing became more difficult. This article seems good witness to White's statement. Here Dewey wants to show an active, developing self; action implies forces or powers and anything he said about developing powers might then be construed to mean independent entities pushing a passive self around. Also, he wanted to show the self striving to meet its needs, to realize its impulses. But again, to speak of self-realization is to be in danger of being interpreted to mean either a natural unfolding, or even worse, the acquisition of more and more of a fixed universal consciousness (perhaps here it was with his earlier self that he struggled for the meaning of words). At any rate, in the discussion of his paper at a Herbart Round Table there were complaints that he did not define his terms. He answered that the purpose of the paper was to redefine his terms, that the cause of the misunderstanding was his refusal to accept arbitrary definitions about which there was no agreement, and that his attempt to reconstruct their meaning was the only way progress could be made toward true conceptions.

27. Dewey, "Interest in Relation to Training of the Will," *Second Supplement*, p. 9.

28. *Ibid.*, p. 19.

29. In the "Psychology of Effort" (*Philosophical Review*, VI [Jan., 1897], 43–56), Dewey argues the case for the sense of effort being sensationally, not spiritually, mediated. Here effort is "nothing more, and also, nothing less, than tension between means and ends in action, and that the sense of effort is the awareness of this conflict" (p. 51). Effort is the critical point in any progress of action, for the only way to make a new coordination is to break up an old one and reconstruct it with a conflicting coordination. The report by the sensation of this conflict constitutes the sense of effort. But if there is mediating interest and motive where ends and means are identified, there is unified activity, complete absorption, free self-expression, and consequently no sense of effort.

30. Dewey, "Interest in Relation to Training of the Will," *Second Supplement*, p. 35.

31. John Dewey, "Imagination and Expression," *Kindergarten Magazine*, IX (Sept., 1896), 63.

32. *Ibid.*

33. There may be plausibility to the notion that the importance Dewey attaches to imagination is a reconstruction of his earlier idealistic view of the two consciousnesses or minds, the individual and the universal. But now the growing imagination is not an absorption of a fixed absolute but an active, simultaneous appropriation and reinterpretation of the culture. Obviously each individual does not build his culture. He is born into it. But it becomes uniquely focused in his imagination. It is no longer man's finiteness that is the obstacle to his attainment of the universal mind; it is the uniqueness of the imagination warped and inhibited by conditions of life that hinders the building of a more common or universal culture.

III: LOGIC

1. John Dewey, "Is Logic a Dualistic Science?" *Open Court,* III (Jan. 16, 1890), 2040–43. "The Logic of Verification," *Open Court,* III (April 24, 1890), 2225–28. "How Do Concepts Arise from Percepts?" *Public School Journal,* XI (Nov., 1891), 128–30. "The Present Position of Logical Theory," *Monist,* II (Oct., 1891), 1–17.

2. John Dewey, "Some Stages of Logical Thought," *Philosophical Review,* IX (Sept., 1900), 465–89.

3. Morton G. White, *The Origin of Dewey's Instrumentalism,* New York: Columbia University Press, 1943, p. 131.

4. *Ibid.,* p. 99.

5. I am indebted to White for this analysis.

6. White, *Origin of Dewey's Instrumentalism,* p. 72.

7. Dewey, "Is Logic a Dualistic Science?" *Open Court,* III (Jan. 16, 1890), p. 2040.

8. Dewey had long opposed formal logic. In his work on Leibniz he had blamed the contradictions of the latter on his use of formal logic.

He had said, "The fundamental contradiction in Leibniz is to be found, I believe, between the method which he adopted—without inquiry into its validity and scope—and the subject-matter, or perhaps better the attitude, to which he attempted to apply this method; between, that is to say, the scholastic formal logic on the

one hand, and the idea of interrelation derived from the development of scientific thought, on the other." (John Dewey, Leibniz's *New Essays Concerning the Human Understanding*, Chicago: S. C. Grigg and Co., 1888, p. 240.)

9. Dewey, "Is Logic a Dualistic Science?" *Open Court*, III (Jan. 16, 1890), p. 2040.

10. *Ibid.*, p. 2041.   11. *Ibid.*   12. *Ibid.*, p. 2042.

13. *Ibid.*

14. It is evident that at this time Dewey is not clear on his explanation of the difference between common sense and science, for he is inconsistent, as is indicated in the following quotations.

In the paper under discussion he says: "Knowledge from the first, whether in the form of ordinary observation or of scientific thinking, is logical; in ordinary observation, however, the logical process is unconscious, dormant, and hence goes easily and inevitably astray. In scientific thinking, the mind knows what it is about; the logical functions are consciously used as guides and as standards." (*Ibid.*, p. 2043.)

But compare this with a statement he makes in "The Present Position of Logical Theory" (*Monist*, II [Oct., 1891], 2), where in discussing the confusion over the true nature and method of science, he says: "Were it otherwise, were there at present a logical theory adequate to the specific and detailed practical results of science, science and scientific men would be conscious of themselves, and would be confident in their work and attitude."

The former position that the difference in the logic of common sense and science is one of conscious as opposed to unconscious processes seems to imply that the scientist first studies logical methods and then knowingly applies them to subject-matter. The second statement implies that the scientist is confused because he does not know the logical processes he follows. This more nearly accords with Dewey's explanation in *Logic: The Theory of Inquiry* (New York, Henry Holt and Co., 1938), in which he takes the position that logical forms accrue to the process of inquiry. There is inquiry involved in both common sense and science. The difference is now a difference of problems.

He says: "The attainment of knowledge of some things is necessarily involved in common sense inquiries, but it occurs for the sake of settlement of some issue of use and enjoyment and not, as in scientific inquiry, for its own sake. In the latter, there is no *direct* involvement of human beings in the *immediate* environment—a fact which carries with it the ground of distinguishing the theoretical from the practical." (*Ibid.,* p. 60.)

In fact, the difference is no longer one of the conscious or unconscious use of logic at all, but is a social problem. He now states: "The difference that now exists between common sense and science is a social, rather than a logical matter. . . . The paths of communication between common sense and science are as yet largely one way lanes. Science takes its departure from common sense, but the return road into common sense is devious and blocked by existing social conditions." (*Ibid.,* p. 77.)

15. Dewey, "Is Logic a Dualistic Science?" *Open Court,* III (Jan. 16, 1890), 2043.

16. This paper by Dewey, "How Do Concepts Arise from Percepts?" appeared with discussions by others in the *Public School Journal,* Vol. XI (1891–92), in what amounted to a debate over the issue of nominalism vs. realism.

George P. Brown gives the general notion of the series of articles. He says they were to be answers to a question posed by W. T. Harris, for the latter the essential question in psychology: "Do concepts originate from percepts positively or negatively?" In other words: "Does the concept originate from the percept by retaining something of the percept and omitting the remnant by abstraction?" or, "Does the concept originate negatively—by dropping limitations or determinations which it received from the object?" (*Ibid.,* p. 28.)

For Dewey the answer did not concern which was real, the particular or the general. It took each to enrich and complete the meaning of the other. W. T. Harris commends Dewey's answer, saying, "The conception thus, as Mr. Dewey tells us, perceives a deeper reality than sense perception." (*Ibid.,* p. 179.)

This is a neat reading of Dewey but I don't believe it is quite what Mr. Dewey said. An interesting contrast, interesting for its educational implications, is the nominalist position of Professor Paul H. Hamus, of Harvard. For him, "The progress from percept to concept is due solely to the repetition of experiences under

varying degrees and circumstances of similarity, and the process of classification has gone on because in each case two successive experiences have been recognized as similar or dissimilar because they have felt the same or because they have felt different." Thus, to teach the concept "West," have the child point west; go to the west edge of the yard; go west two or three blocks; go west to the nearby range of hills. (*Ibid.*, p. 233.)

17. Dewey, "How Do Concepts Arise from Percepts?" *Public School Journal*, XI (1891–92), 128.

18. *Ibid.*

19. By the use of an incomplete quotation, I believe that White is wrong in accusing Dewey of an error in thinking at this point.

White quotes this passage where Dewey is speaking of a particular percept, that of a triangle: "Knowledge of it from this point of view would be exhausted in getting its exact shape, size, length of sides, degrees of angles, stuff made of, color, etc. The mind would no where be led beyond the consideration of the bare thing present. Even if it were found that the sum of its three interior angles was equal to two right angles, this would be a trait of the particular triangle, a bare item of information of no more general value than that the length of one side was 12/17 inches."

White comments that Dewey is wrong here, for "We know that the trait concerning the sum of the angles is characteristic of all triangles, whereas having one side's length to be 12/17 inches is not." (White, *The Origin of Dewey's Instrumentalism*, p. 68.)

While this is true, as no doubt Dewey was aware, he was denying generality to the fact that the sum of the angles of a triangle was equal to two right angles *as a mere percept*.

"This point of view" in the opening sentence of White's quotation above refers to a preceding statement of Dewey's: "For example, take the percept of a triangle. So far as this is a mere percept, it is regarded wholly as a particular thing." (Dewey, "How Do Concepts Arise from Percepts?" *Public School Journal*, XI [Nov., 1891], p. 128.)

It is clear that Dewey is denying the questioned generality as a percept, not as ultimately untrue.

20. Dewey, "How Do Concepts Arise from Percepts?" *Public School Journal*, XI (Nov., 1891), 128.

21. Dewey, "The Logic of Verification," *Open Court*, IV (April 24, 1890), 2225–28.

22. *Ibid.*, p. 2227.   23. *Ibid.*   24. *Ibid.*

25. Dewey, "The Present Position of Logical Theory," *Monist*, II (Oct., 1891), 1–17.

26. *Ibid.*, p. 3.

27. Dewey here shows the consistency of scholasticism in its proper context; its inconsistency with what modern scientists do. He says: "To examine the *material*, to test its truth: to suppose that intelligence could cut loose from this body of authority dogmatic fact, tradition, revelation and go straight to nature, to history itself, to find the truth; to build up a free and independent science—to this point of incoherency mediaeval scholasticism never attained. To proclaim freedom of thought, the rejection of all external authority, the right and the power of thought to get at truth for itself, and yet continue to define thought as a faculty apart from fact, was reserved for modern enlightenment." (*Ibid.*, p. 5.)

Later, in his *Logic: The Theory of Inquiry*, Dewey makes the same point and adds that the very consistency of Aristotelianism and Scholasticism in its own context is proof of its inconsistency in the present situation.

28. Dewey, "The Present Position of Logical Theory," *Monist*, II (Oct., 1891), 6.

29. *Ibid.*, p. 9.

30. Dewey, "Some Stages of Logical Thought," *Philosophical Review*, IX (Sept., 1900), 489.

31. *Ibid.*, p. 488.   32. *Ibid.*, p. 465.   33. *Ibid.*, p. 468.

34. In the history of the race this stage may be seen in the case of the Hebrew judge who governed conduct by seeing that particular cases conformed to existent laws. As the prophet replaced the judge and emphasized the right-mindedness that enabled each individual to see the law in each case for himself, so does the first stage of thought, fixed ideas, give way to the second stage, discussion.

35. Dewey, "Some Stages of Logical Thought," *Philosophical Review*, IX (Sept., 1900), 472.

36. It was the Sophists who emphasized the loss of assurance; they extended it to include all ideas as ideas, as having no inherent value because they were based upon prejudice, interest, or arbitrary choice.

37. Dewey, "Some Stages of Logical Thought," *Philosophical Review*, IX (Sept., 1900), 473.

38. That these stages of thought were not fixed stages, once passed through forever gone, is shown by Dewey when he says modern empiricists have been similarly guilty of wholesale depreciation of reflection. The stage in actual dominance at a given period of history both reflects and effects social conditions. The empiricists of Dewey's time may be thought of as reflecting a nominalism growing out of a loss of assurance in a "common denominator" due to the rapidly changing conditions of life; and they may have effected an acceleration of this trend. While the scientific stage of inquiry represents the highest point in the development of thought, it may need the support of the third stage if it is not to fall back into the second. I believe it is possible to make a case for the notion that any stages Dewey may have had in his system of education are related to this point. The first period of education may be thought of as a stage for the building of a common perspective to support scientific thought as the focus of a second stage of education.

Involved here, again, is the relation between common sense and science. We have seen that Dewey substituted "social conditions" for "lack of consciousness" as an explanation of the barriers between common sense and science. Another way, then, to state the stages of education may be first, the development of common sense in formulating the problems of social conditions where consciousness of *that* method may be essential, and the development of scientific inquiry into solution of the problems—the latter, problems, being the connecting link both between the stages of education and between common sense and science.

39. Dewey, "Some Stages of Logical Thought," *Philosophical Review*, IX (Sept., 1900), 475.

40. *Ibid.*, p. 480.   41. *Ibid.*, p. 483.   42. *Ibid.*, p. 484.

43. *Ibid.*, p 487.

44. John Dewey, *Studies in Logical Theory*, Chicago: University of Chicago Press, 1903.

45. *Ibid.*, p. 12.   46. *Ibid.*, p. 10.   47. *Ibid.*, p. 19.

48. *Ibid.*, p. 22.

49. It is at this point that Dewey's uncertainty, at the time, regarding the barrier btween common sense and science does not permit a clear interpretation of the implication of his theory for education. For if it is lack of consciousness that differentiates common sense from science, the fact would seem to imply an education for the development of the required consciousness. But if social conditions block the relation between science and common sense, then the implication would seem to be that education must focus not only upon consciousness of method but also upon the content of these social conditions and problems.

IV: ETHICS

1. John Dewey, *Outlines of a Critical Theory of Ethics*, Ann Arbor: Register Publishing Co., 1891, p. 33.

2. *Ibid.*, p. 52.   3. *Ibid.*, p. 54.   4. *Ibid.*, p. 56.

5. *Ibid.*, p. 66.   6. *Ibid.*, p. 70.   7. *Ibid.*, p. 71.

8. *Ibid.*, p. 77.   9. *Ibid.*, p. 88.   10. *Ibid.*, p. 97.

11. *Ibid.*, p. 101.   12. *Ibid.*, p. 104.

13. Dewey makes a very interesting comment at this point. He says: "There is a tendency in the present emphasis on altruism to erect the principle of charity, in a sense which implies continual social inequality, and social slavery, or undue dependence of one upon another, into a fundamental moral principle. It is well to 'do good' to others, but it is much better to do this by securing for them the freedom which makes it possible for them to get along in the future without such 'altruism' from others." (*Ibid.*, p. 108.)

14. *Ibid.*, p. 114.

15. Dewey does not ignore the meaning to the artisan of wealth and reputation for himself, or the use and benefit of his work to others. In so far as his work is a means merely to these ends, it

loses much of its significance. But to the extent that the thought of these effects is bound up, or intrinsic, in relation with his self-respect in workmanship, it intensifies and enlarges the content of his interest, and increases the meaning and moral quality of his activities.

16. Dewey, *Outlines of a Critical Theory of Ethics*, p. 150.

17. *Ibid.*, p. 131.   18. *Ibid.*, p. 190.

19. John Dewey, "Moral Theory and Practice," *International Journal of Ethics*, I (Jan., 1891), 191.

20. *Ibid.*, p. 196.   21. *Ibid.*, p. 203.

22. John Dewey, "Green's Theory of the Moral Motive," *Philosophical Review*, I (Nov., 1892), 593–612.

23. John Dewey, "Self-Realization as the Moral Ideal," *Philosophical Review*, II (Nov., 1893), 652–64.

24. This mention of theological ethics indicates that Dewey was disturbed in regard to the adequacy of religious morals to serve as guides in particular situations. Yet he did not directly express his attitude toward theological ethics at this time. It is interesting to speculate upon the reasons for this omission. Two possibilities come to mind. One follows from the fact that his views were radical in respect to all existing ethical views and he desired as intelligent consideration of them as he could get. He may have felt that the emotional sanction accompanying theological ethics would possibly have prevented this. In the second place, he was concerned about the ethics of the everyday, working, and suffering life of humanity—with problems of conduct within political, industrial, economic, and social arrangements which were in a state of flux due to the advance of science and technology. Many of the moral precepts sanctioned by religion, such as honesty, truthfulness, respect for life, either were not in general question themselves, or were quite worthy if they could be held in proper relation to the concrete affairs of life. Others may have been so aloof from the mundane affairs that he may not have considered them in the immediate arena of conflict.

25. Dewey, "Self-Realization as the Moral Ideal," *Philosophical Review*, II (Nov., 1893), 663.

26. John Dewey, *The Study of Ethics: A Syllabus,* Ann Arbor: Register Publishing Co., 1894, p. 40.

27. *Ibid.,* p. 35.   28. *Ibid.,* p. 36.

29. In 1896, in "The Metaphysical Method in Ethics" (*Psychological Review,* III, 181-88), Dewey, in criticizing D'Arcy's attempt to find a metaphysical foundation for ethics, says that such foundations require more grounding themselves than does the ethical superstructure they try to support, and that ethical theory needs adequate psychological and social method, not metaphysical support.

30. Dewey, *Study of Ethics: A Syllabus,* p. 11.

31. *Ibid.,* p. 14.   32. *Ibid.,* p. 22.   33. *Ibid.,* p. 69.

34. *Ibid.,* p. 71.   35. *Ibid.,* p. 4.

36. John Dewey, "The Evolutionary Method as Applied to Morality. I. Its Scientific Necessity," *Philosophical Review,* XI (March, 1902), 107–24; "II. Its Significance for Conduct," *Philosophical Review,* XI (July, 1902), 353–71.

37. Dewey, "The Evolutionary Method as Applied to Morality. II. Its Significance for Conduct," *Philosophical Review,* XI (July, 1902), 356.

38. *Ibid.,* p. 360.   39. *Ibid.,* p. 366.   40. *Ibid.,* p. 371.

41. Reprinted in John Dewey, *Problems of Men,* New York: Philosophical Library, 1946, pp. 211–49.

42. *Ibid.,* p. 248.

43. There was considerable agreement among educators of the time that the four important moral habits were regularity, punctuality, silence, and industry.

W. T. Harris said, in "The Relation of School Discipline to Moral Education" (*Third Yearbook of the National Herbart Society,* Chicago: University of Chicago Press, 1897, p. 72), "Lax discipline in a school saps the moral character of the pupil. It allows him to work merely as he pleases, and he will not reinforce his feeble will by regularity, punctuality, and systematic industry. He grows up in habits of whispering and other species of intermeddling with his fellow pupils: neither doing what is reasonable for himself nor allowing others to do it."

Charles DeGarmo, writing on "Social Aspects of Moral Education," in the same source, opposes this strictly individual approach and says the school must become a social institution. But, even

for him, it is still an institution apart from life, with its own necessary morality among which are these same four habits.

44. While Dewey opposes the use of punishment per se, as a motive, there is a place for it in his ethics. He says: "There is the use of punishment to draw positive attention to content otherwise ignored—punishment as a means of enforcing an idea not strong enough to make its own way in an immature mind . . . punishment, in the case say of a lie, is morally effective just in the degree in which fear of it does not operate as an isolated motive, but is the emphasis required to bring out the undesirable quality of the act itself." (*Study of Ethics: A Syllabus,* p. 118.)

45. When the intuitive and hedonistic theories are combined we reach the height of practical confusion, Dewey believes:

"Present methods seem to take both the intuitive and utilitarian positions in their extreme forms, and then attempt the combination of both. It is virtually assumed that prior to instruction the child knows well enough what he should and should not do; that his acts have a conscious moral quality from the first; it is also assumed, to a large extent, that only by appeal to external punishment and rewards can the child be got to see any reason for doing the right and avoiding the wrong. Now these two propositions are so related that they cannot possibly both be true." ("The Chaos in Moral Training," *Popular Science Monthly,* XLV [Aug., 1894], 441.)

On second thought Dewey adds that on one basis the two propositions could be true—total depravity.

V: SOCIAL PHILOSOPHY

1. John Dewey, "Ethics and Physical Science," *Andover Review,* VII (June, 1887), 580.

2. *Ibid.,* p. 582. With the reading of the papers written by Dewey during this formative period of his thinking there comes the notion that he erected his theories with constant reference to this basic position and that he never committed the "original sin" of ignoring it. It is possible that inconsistencies may be found in his logic, psychology, ethics, etc., but no part of his theories are

inconsistent with his devotion to humanity. Those who find fault with his logic, who claim inadequacies in his psychology, who have a distaste for his ethics, who see weaknesses in his educational ideas, or in any other way seek to discredit his thinking, will be on firmer ground if they too make this same check for their criticisms and interpretations.

3. John Dewey, *The Ethics of Democracy*, University of Michigan, Philosophical Papers, Second Series, No. 1, Ann Arbor: Andrews and Company, 1888, p. 1.

4. *Ibid.*, p. 2.

5. John Dewey, "Two Phases of Renan's Life: The Faith of 1850 and the Doubt of 1890," *Open Court*, VI (Dec. 29, 1892), 3505.

6. John Dewey, "Renan's Loss of Faith in Science," *Open Court*, VII (Jan. 5, 1893), 3513.

7. Dewey explains Renan's later loss of faith in science as a "social motor," by pointing to "the intrenched class interest which resists all attempts of science to take practical form and become a 'social motor.' When we remember that every forward step of science has involved readjustment of institutional life, that even such an apparently distant region as the solar system could not be annexed to scientific inquiry without arousing the opposing force of the mightiest political organization of the day; when we recall such things it is not surprising that the advance of scientific method to the matters closest to man—his social relationships—should have gone on more slowly than was expected. The resistance from the powers whose existence is threatened by such advance has not become less effective in becoming more direct and subtle." (*Ibid.*, p. 3515.)

8. *Ibid.*, p. 3513.   9. *Ibid.*, p. 3514.   10. *Ibid.*

11. Dewey, "Ethics and Physical Science," *Andover Review*, VII (June, 1887), 585.

12. Dewey, *The Ethics of Democracy*, p. 17.

13. *Ibid.*, p. 18.   14. *Ibid.*, p. 21.   15. *Ibid.*, p. 23.

16. *Ibid.*, p. 24.

17. In a review of *Philosophy and Political Economy in Some of Their Historical Relations*, by James Bonar, Dewey criticizes Bonar for his judgment in selecting authors for review. Bonar

gives an account of the economic content found in many philosophic writers, yet he hardly mentions Rousseau. And Dewey comments, "Yet surely it was Rousseau, more than any other writer, who brought to consciousness the position of the economic forces in social organization as such, and the place of the economic problem in the whole social and political problem." (*Political Science Quarterly*, IX [Dec. 1894], 741–44.)

Dewey goes on to insist that the theory which assigns economic needs and struggles as the determining force in the evolution of all institutions is too important as a doctrine and too evident in practice to be overlooked.

18. Dewey, *The Ethics of Democracy*, p. 25.

19. *Ibid.*, p. 26.   20. *Ibid.*   21. *Ibid.*, p. 27.

22. John Dewey, "Austin's Theory of Sovereignty," *Political Science Quarterly*, IX (March, 1894), 31–52.

23. *Ibid.*, p. 51.   24. *Ibid.*, p. 52.

25. In regard to ultimate goals, Dewey comments: "It is of great advantage to the individual to be aware of what he really is about in a special case, and any principle, however formal and abstract, which aids him in doing this is justified thereby. But it is not the *remote* goal, but simply a larger view of the present, which thus helps one. It is the reference of an act to the present society which it maintains and furthers that helps one see its true content; not its reference to a society distant an infinite length of time." ("The Metaphysical Method in Ethics," *Psychological Review*, III [March, 1896], 187.)

26. Merle Curti, *The Social Ideas of American Educators*, New York: Chas. Scribner's Sons, 1935, p. 508.

27. John Dewey, "Galton's Statistical Methods," *Publications of the American Statistical Association*, New Series, I (Sept., 1889), 334.

28. John Dewey, "Psychology and Social Practice," *Psychological Review*, VII (March, 1900), 111.

29. John Dewey, "Evolutionary Method as Applied to Morality," *Psychological Review*, XI (July, 1902), 362.

30. John Dewey, *School and Society*, Chicago: The University of Chicago Press, 1900.

31. *Ibid.*, p. 21.   32. *Ibid.*, p. 22.   33. *Ibid.*, p. 24.

34. *Ibid.,* p. 25.

35. Nor, it might be added, between the world of men and the world of women. Dewey recognizes the discrimination against women in "Health and Sex in Higher Education." He reports a study of the traditional notion that women's health will not permit the rigors of education. He finds little to substantiate the claim and points out that while a few women receive a vocational training, nothing is done about women's *education.* (*Popular Science Monthly,* XXVIII [March, 1886], 606–14.)

Dewey makes another interesting comment in his review of Ward's *The Psychic Factors of Civilization.* He describes Ward's statement of the difference between male and female intuition. Whereas the male intuition develops in regard to reaching remote ends, the female, more concerned with immediate problems of protection for herself and her young against dangers, develops intuition with reference to means. When Ward says this is what makes male intelligence radical and female intelligence conservative, Dewey disagrees; for, he says, male intelligence may be radical as to ends, conservative as to means, while female intelligence is the reverse.

Then he says, "The prevalent theory of the essentially conservative nature of women's intelligence seems to me a fiction of the male intelligence maintained in order to keep this inconvenient radicalism of women in check." ("Social Psychology," *Psychological Review,* I [July, 1894], 407.)

VII: DEWEY'S REACTIONS TO
OTHER EDUCATIONAL MOVEMENTS
OF THE TIME

1. The justification for the association of W. T. Harris with traditional education is made apparent in the later section devoted to this topic.

2. Charles DeGarmo, "Most Pressing Problems (1895) Concerning the Elementary Course of Study," in *First Yearbook of the Herbart Society for the Scientific Study of Teaching,* Bloomington, Illinois, 1895, pp. 7–27.

3. Frank M. McMurry, "Concentration," in *First Yearbook of the Herbart Society for the Scientific Study of Teaching*, p. 29.

4. There were many discussions among the Herbartians over the question of the most suitable name for this element of the apperception theory. The words concentration, coordination, and correlation were given subtle distinctions pointing to equality among subjects, subordination of one to another, or to sequence and organization; but they were all used to convey the idea of some associative relationship among ideas.

5. McMurry, "Concentration," in *First Yearbook of the Herbart Society for the Scientific Study of Teaching*, p. 30.

6. *Ibid.*, p. 61.

7. Sarah C. Brooks, "Discussion," in *First Supplement, First Yearbook of the Herbart Society for the Scientific Study of Teaching*, Bloomington, Illinois, 1895, p. 149.

8. Louis H. Galbreath, "Discussion," in *First Supplement, First Yearbook of the Herbart Society for the Scientific Study of Teaching*, p. 164.

9. *Ibid.*, p. 165.

10. John Dewey, "Interpretation of the Culture-Epoch Theory," *Public School Journal*, XV (Jan., 1896), 233–36.

11. I believe that Dewey was either too emphatic here, or too considerate of his colleagues in the society to charge them with inconsistency. Actually, C. C. Van Liew *did* think of correspondence in this way, for he said: "We must insist, then, that we are dealing in this comparison, not with the products of development, but with the development of mental functions that have brought about the products." ("Educational Theory of Culture Epochs," in *First Yearbook of the Herbart Society for the Scientific Study of Teaching*, p. 98.) However, in applying the theory he usually thought in terms of products.

12. Dewey, "Interpretation of the Culture-Epoch Theory," *Public School Journal*, XV (Jan., 1896), 235.

13. *Ibid.*, p. 236.

14. John Dewey, "Interpretation of Savage Mind," *Psychological Review*, IX (May, 1902), 217.

15. *Ibid.*, p. 219.   16. *Ibid.*, p. 229.

17. C. C. Van Liew, "Child Study as Related to Instruction,"

Transactions of the Illinois Society for Child-Study, I, No. 1 (1894), 9.

18. John Dewey, "Criticisms, Wise and Otherwise, on Modern Child-Study," in *National Education Association, Addresses and Proceedings,* 1897, pp. 867–68.

19. *Ibid.,* p. 868.

20. John Dewey, "The Interpretation Side of Child-Study," *Transactions of the Illinois Society for Child-Study,* II, No. 2 (1897), 17–27.

21. *Ibid.,* p. 18.   22. *Ibid.,* p. 20.   23. *Ibid.,* p. 22.

24. *Ibid.,* p. 23.   25. *Ibid.,* p. 27.

26. Arthur B. Mays, "The Concept of Vocational Education in the Thinking of the General Educator, 1845 to 1945," *University of Illinois Bulletin,* Vol. 43, No. 65 (July, 1946).

27. *Ibid.,* p. 36.   28. *Ibid.,* p. 53.

29. John Dewey, "Review of Katherine Elizabeth Dopp, *The Place of Industries in Elementary Education,*" *Elementary School Teacher,* III (June, 1903), 728.

30. John Dewey, "Current problems in Secondary Education," *School Review* (Jan., 1902), p. 24.

31. *Ibid.,* p. 26.

32. Dewey, "Review of Katherine Elizabeth Dopp, *The Place of Industries in Elementary Education,*" *Elementary School Teacher,* III (June, 1903), 727.

33. John Dewey, "Review of Harris, *Psychologic Foundations of Education,*" *Educational Review,* XVI (June, 1898), 1–14.

34. *Ibid.,* p. 8.   35. *Ibid.,* p. 12.

36. Dewey makes this interesting comment: "The early mental attitude of the child is in a way closely akin to philosophic interest. It is of course crude and naive; but the natural bent of attention is toward function, aim, moving spirit, rather than toward particulars." (*Ibid.*) There is quite a distance between this view and that which holds that but few adults *can* ever attain the philosophic view, which, perhaps, helps to explain why so few *do.*

37. *Ibid.,* p. 13.   38. *Ibid.*   39. *Ibid.,* p. 14.

VII: THE THEORY OF SCHOOLING

1. Katherine Camp Mayhew and Anna Camp Edwards, *The Dewey School*, New York: Appleton-Century Co., 1936, p. 465.

2. *Ibid.*   3. *Ibid.*

4. Dewey may have made two assumptions here which the fate of his theories in subsequent interpretations prove not to have been justified. In the first place, he stated that the fact of great social change brought about by the development of science and technology, with all of the resulting bewilderment and confusion in social life, was so obvious that even he who runs might see it. It seems evident now that many, even, of those who walk have yet to grasp the import of this reality. In the second place, while he added the insight that a complete view of democracy included the principle that all men must share in the creation of the good life, his assumption that most men agreed that all should share in the products of the good life may well have been overly optimistic.

5. Actually, in most of the references previously cited in our discussion of the foundational disciplines and the other educational movements of the time, Dewey makes some explicit comment, either in passing or directly to the point, in regard to the social situation. It is, then, the total effect of all of his papers written during this formative period which supports the statement of his social diagnosis given here. However, the following sources are among those supplying the principal content of his social analysis:

The Ethics of Democracy, University of Michigan, Philosophical Papers, Second Series, No. 1, Ann Arbor: Andrews and Co., 1888, 28 pp.

Outlines of a Critical Theory of Ethics, Ann Arbor: Register Publishing Co., 1891, 253 pp.

"Moral Theory and Practice," *International Journal of Ethics*, I (Jan., 1891), 186–203.

"Poetry and Philosophy," *Andover Review*, XVI (Aug., 1891), 105–16.

"Two Phases of Renan's Life: The Faith of 1850 and the Doubt of 1890," *Open Court*, VI (Dec., 1892), 3505–6.

"Renan's Loss of Faith in Science," *Open Court*, VII (Jan., 1893), 3512–15.

The Study of Ethics: A Syllabus, Ann Arbor: Register Publishing Co., 1894, 151 pp.

"Social Psychology," *Psychological Review,* I (July, 1894), 400–411.

The School and Society, Chicago: University of Chicago Press, 1899, 125 pp.

"Psychology and Social Practice," *Psychological Review,* VII (March, 1900), 105–24.

"The Primary Education Fetich," *Forum,* XXV (May, 1898), 315–28.

6. John Dewey, *The Child and the Curriculum,* Chicago: University of Chicago Press, 1902, p. 2.

Since in much of his thinking during this period Dewey kept foremost the problem of education, many of his writings previously cited support the view of his theory of schooling as given here. However, basic sources pertinent to his theory of schooling, in addition to *The Child and the Curriculum,* are:

The School and Society, Chicago: The University of Chicago Press, 1889, 125 pp.

The Elementary School Record, Chicago: The University of Chicago Press, 1900, 232 pp.

"Ethical Principles Underlying Education," in *Third Yearbook of the National Herbart Society,* 1897, pp. 7–34.

The Educational Situation, Chicago: The University of Chicago Press, 1902, 104 pp.

"Are the Schools Doing What the People Want Them to Do?" *Educational Review,* XXI (May, 1901), 459–74.

"The School as Social Center," in *National Education Association, Addresses and Proceedings,* 1902, pp. 373–83.

VIII: THE LABORATORY SCHOOL

1. For a complete account of the Dewey School, see Katherine Camp Mayhew and Anna Camp Edwards, *The Dewey School,* New York: D. Appleton-Century Co., 1936.

2. *Ibid.,* p. 81.   3. *Ibid.,* p. 377.

4. *Ibid.*   5. *Ibid.,* p. 9.

6. Dewey has expressed the opinion that perhaps the leader-

ship of the inexperienced was not sufficiently positive and that too much responsibility was placed upon teachers.

He has said: "In avoiding hard and fast plans to be executed and dictation of methods to be followed, individual teachers were, if anything, not given enough assistance either in advance or by way of critical supervision." (Mayhew and Edwards, *The Dewey School*, p. 366.)

Yet he adds that it is better to err in this direction rather than "in that of too definite formulation of syllabi and elaboration in advance of methods used in teaching and discipline. Whatever else was lost, vitality and constant growth were gained." (*Ibid.*)

In this connection, a constant visitor to the school remarked: "Mr. Dewey had the greatest real faith of any educator I have known in the classroom teacher's judgment as to what children can and should do." (*Ibid.*)

7. John Dewey, *The Child and the Curriculum*, Chicago: The University of Chicago Press, 1902, p. 18.

8. Mayhew and Edwards, *The Dewey School*, p. 45.

9. From the experimentation and interpretations of group interests there came to be recognized three stages, or periods, in the life of the child's interests and abilities. The first extends from the age of four to about eight or eight-and-a-half years. In this stage, the children are largely concerned with direct social activities of doing and telling. In the second stage, from about eight to ten, the growing complexity of their activities give rise to more conscious concern over methods of doing and telling. The children are ready to give attention to form and technique in reading, writing, numbers, handwork, and science. In the third period, through the thirteenth year, interests turn more toward utilizing skills in problems of investigation, reflection, and generalization. There is also a turn toward greater differentiation and specialization of individual interests. "If the first period has given the child a common and varied background, if the second has introduced him to the control of reading, writing, numbering, manipulating materials, etc., as instruments of inquiry, he is now ready in the third for a certain amount of specialization without danger of isolation or artificiality." (Mayhew and Edwards, *The Dewey School*, p. 54.)

There was no conception of these stages as representing distinct breaks; rather a gradual transition was seen, best denoted as a growing ability to relate means and ends in widening relationships and as discipline in securing and using adequate means to attain the end at the expense of immediate satisfaction in less worthy ends.

10. Mayhew and Edwards, *The Dewey School*, p. 49.

11. *Ibid.*, p. 194.   12. *Ibid.*

13. Dewey, *The Child and the Curriculum*, p. 22.

14. *Ibid.*, p. 30.

15. Mayhew and Edwards, *The Dewey School*, p. 372.

16. *Ibid.*, p. 36.

17. John Dewey, *The School and Society*, Chicago: The University of Chicago Press, 1899, p. 45.

18. Mayhew and Edwards, *The Dewey School*, p. 63.

19. *Ibid.*, p. 337.

20. It may be held that the technique of suggestion was no more than a disguised name for dictation, albeit kindly and benevolent; it may be held that children are wont, especially at an early age, to accept the suggestions of teachers as their own, and therefore actually followed directions imposed from above. As with any technique, skill in making suggestions had to be acquired through experience, and no doubt it was possible, even probable, that there was some improper use of the technique. But the distinctive and saving feature in the use of the skill in the Dewey School was the fact that its application was guided by the underlying theory. Hence the teachers were alert to, and carefully interpretive of, the children's reactions to suggestions. True, the teachers had preferences; they wanted the children's interests to expand in fruitful channels. But if the teachers' reading of the children's behavior and attitudes indicated that the children did not grasp the suggestions as related to their intrinsic interests, the matter was dropped or postponed until the children indicated they sensed its appropriateness.

21. Mayhew and Edwards, *The Dewey School*, p. 345.

22. *Ibid.*, p. 338.

23. Dewey, *The School and Society*, p. 55.

24. Mayhew and Edwards, *The Dewey School*, p. 361.

25. Dewey, *The School and Society*, p. 56.

26. Mayhew and Edwards, *The Dewey School*, p. 305.

27. *Ibid.*, p. 213.

28. In this instance, it was found that the interest of these boys in science was related to their work in shop where they were making surveying and navigating instruments. Continuity with the group enterprise was then sought through this channel, rather than through the historical approach.

29. Mayhew and Edwards, *The Dewey School*, p. 421.

30. *Ibid.*

31. Dewey, *The School and Society*, p. 13.

32. Mayhew and Edwards, *The Dewey School*, p. 422.

33. *Ibid.*, p. 424.   34. *Ibid.*, p. 382.   35. *Ibid.*, p. 422.

IX: AN ASSESSMENT OF DEWEY'S THEORY OF SCHOOLING

1. John Dewey, *A Common Faith*, New Haven: Yale University Press, 1934.

2. Harold Rugg, *Foundations for American Education*, New York: World Book Co., 1947, p. 546.

3. John Dewey, *Art as Experience*, New York: Minton, Balch and Co., 1935.

4. Katherine Camp Mayhew and Anna Camp Edwards, *The Dewey School*, New York: D. Appleton-Century Co., 1945, p. 465.

5. *Ibid.*, pp. xv, 465.

6. It is conceivable that one phase of reconstruction of Dewey's theory of schooling may eventually focus upon the integrating role of occupations in human life. Dewey has emphasized the development of art and knowledge, values and ideals, out of man's basic struggle for equilibrium in the physical world. With man's growing conquest over nature by means of the twin forces of science and technology, there have come visions of a time when this struggle, so fierce in the past experience of the human race, may be all but eliminated, or at least so one-sided in favor of man's inventiveness that the matrix from which the latter emerged will have lost its integrating significance. In this case, reconstruction would include a search for a new core of human experience.

However, the present conditions of life remain such as to suggest that the efforts of this generation to solve the problem of education must continue to concentrate on the place of occupations in the development of ethical life. The notion advanced, though, does imply that we might fruitfully look forward as well as backward in inquiry into a principle for the integration of experience.

7. Mayhew and Edwards, *The Dewey School*, pp. 467–71. In reflecting upon the significance of these difficulties, it may be well to consider the fact that just now, fifty years later, are we beginning to make much headway in the development of organismic, social psychological data, in the formulation of a theory and related procedures for democratic leadership and group processes, and in the development of resource material for the content of a schooling conceived as an experiment in democratic living.

8. *Ibid.*, p. 473.   9. *Ibid.*, p. 396.   10. *Ibid.*, p. 464.

11. Dewey, *The School and Society*, Chicago: The University of Chicago Press, 1899, p. 83. (My italics.)

12. *Ibid.*, p. 27.

13. Harold Rugg, for example, takes this view: "Mahew and Edwards assembled scattered comments on the success of the School made by visiting educators, parents, and former pupils—'thirty years after.' But these are all pro-Dewey and so far as I can see contribute nothing to the needed critical appraisal of the educational product. Students of educational reconstruction will regret, I am sure, that the Dewey group did not conduct a *systematic and objective inquiry* into the traceable effects of the school's work in the later lives of its graduates." (*Foundations for American Education*, p. 556.)

14. Mayhew and Edwards, *The Dewey School, passim.*

15. See footnote 45, Chapter IV.

BIBLIOGRAPHY

WORKS BY JOHN DEWEY

"The New Psychology," *Andover Review*, II (September, 1884), 278–89.

"The Psychological Standpoint," *Mind*, XI (January, 1886), 1–19.

"Health and Sex in Higher Education," *Popular Science Monthly*, XXVIII (March, 1886), 606–14.

"Psychology as Philosophic Method," *Mind*, XI (April, 1886), 153–73.

Psychology. Third revised edition. New York: Harper and Brothers, 1891. Pp. xii + 427.

"Ethics and Physical Science," *Andover Review*, VII (June, 1887), 573–91.

Leibniz's New Essays Concerning the Human Understanding. A Critical Exposition. Chicago: S. C. Griggs and Company, 1888. Pp. xvii + 272.

The Ethics of Democracy. University of Michigan, Philosophical Papers, Second Series, No. 1. Ann Arbor: Andrews and Company, 1888. Pp. 28.

"The Philosophy of Thomas Hill Green," *Andover Review*, XI (April, 1889), 337–55.

"Galton's Statistical Methods," *Publications of the American Statistical Association*, I (September, 1889), 331–34.

"On Some Current Conceptions of the Term 'Self,'" *Mind*, XV (January, 1890), 58–74.

"Is Logic a Dualistic Science?" *Open Court*, III (January, 1890), 2040–43.

"The Logic of Verification," *Open Court*, IV (April, 1890), 2225–28.

Outlines of a Critical Theory of Ethics. Ann Arbor: Register Publishing Company, 1891. Pp. viii + 253.

"Moral Theory and Practice," *International Journal of Ethics*, I (January, 1891), 186–203.

"Review of James Hutchins Baker, *Elementary Psychology, with*

*Practical Applications to Education and the Conduct of Life,"
    Educational Review*, I (May, 1891), 495–96.

"Poetry and Philosophy," *Andover Review*, XVI (August, 1891),
    105–16.

"The Present Position of Logical Theory," *Monist*, II (October,
    1891), 1–17.

"How Do Concepts Arise from Percepts?" *Public School Journal*,
    XI (November, 1891), 128–30.

"Green's Theory of the Moral Motive," *Philosophical Review*, I
    (November, 1892), 593–612.

"Two Phases of Renan's Life: The Faith of 1850 and the Doubt of
    1890," *Open Court*, VI (December, 1892), 3505–6.

"Renan's Loss of Faith in Science," *Open Court*, VII (January,
    1893), 3512–15.

"The Superstition of Necessity," *Monist*, III (April, 1893), 362–79.

"Teaching Ethics in the High School," *Educational Review*, VI
    (November, 1893), 313–21.

"Self-Realization as the Moral Ideal," *Philosophical Review*, II
    (November, 1893), 652–64.

The Study of Ethics: A Syllabus. Ann Arbor: Register Publishing
    Company, 1894. Pp. iv + 151.

"The Psychology of Infant Language," *Psychological Review*, I
    (January, 1894), 63–66.

"Austin's Theory of Sovereignty," *Political Science Quarterly*, IX
    (March, 1894), 31–52.

"The Ego as Cause," *Philosophical Review*, III (May, 1894), 337–
    41.

"Social Psychology," *Psychological Review*, I (July, 1894), 400–411.

"The Chaos in Moral Training," *Popular Science Monthly*, XLV
    (August, 1894), 433–43.

"The Theory of Emotion. I. Emotional Attitudes," *Psychological
    Review*, II (November, 1894), 553–69.

"The Theory of Emotion. II. The Significance of Emotions,"
    Psychological Review, II (January, 1895), 13–32.

"Review of James Bonar, *Philosophy and Political Economy in
    Some of Their Historical Relations*," *Political Science Quarterly*,
    IX (December, 1894), 741–44.

"The Results of Child-Study Applied to Education," *Transactions*

of the *Illinois Society for Child-Study*, I, No. 4 (January, 1895), 18–19.

"Interest as Related to the Training of the Will," in National Herbart Society, Second Supplement to the Herbart Yearbook for 1895. Bloomington, Illinois, 1896, pp. 209–55.

"Interpretation of the Culture-Epoch Theory," *Public School Journal*, XV (January, 1896), 233–36.

"The Reflex Arc Concept in Psychology," *Psychological Review*, III (July, 1896), 357–70.

"Influence of the High School upon Educational Methods," *School Review*, IV (January, 1896), 1–12.

"The Metaphysical Method in Ethics," *Psychological Review*, III (March, 1896), 181–88.

"A Pedagogical Experiment," *Kindergarten Magazine*, VIII (June, 1896), 739–41.

"Imagination and Expression," *Kindergarten Magazine*, IX (September, 1896), 61–69.

"Ethical Principles Underlying Education," in National Herbart Society, Third Yearbook. Chicago, 1897, pp. 7–34.

"The Kindergarten and Child-Study," in National Education Association, Addresses and Proceedings, 1897, pp. 585–86.

"Criticisms, Wise and Otherwise, on Modern Child-Study," in National Education Association, Addresses and Proceedings, 1897, pp. 867–68.

"The Psychology of Effort," *Philosophical Review*, VI (January, 1897), 43–56.

"The Psychological Aspect of the School Curriculum," *Educational Review*, XIII (April, 1897), 356–69.

"The Interpretation Side of Child-Study," *Transactions of the Illinois Society for Child-Study*, II, No. 2 (July, 1897), 17–27.

"Evolution and Ethics," *Monist*, VIII (April, 1898), 321–41.

"The Primary Education Fetich," *Forum*, XXV (May, 1898), 315–28.

"Review of William Torrey Harris, *Psychologic Foundations of Education*," *Educational Review*, XVI (June, 1898), 1–14.

"Review of James Mark Baldwin, *Social and Ethical Interpretations in Mental Development*," *Philosophical Review*, VII (July, 1898), 398–409.

The School and Society. Chicago: The University of Chicago Press, 1899. Pp. 125.

"Play and Imagination in Relation to Early Education," *Kindergarten Magazine*, XI (June, 1899), 636–40.

"Principles of Mental Development as Illustrated in Early Infancy," *Transactions of the Illinois Society for Child-Study*, IV (October, 1899), 65–83.

The Elementary School Record. Chicago: The University of Chicago Press, 1900. Pp. 232.

"Psychology and Social Practice," *Psychological Review*, VII (March, 1900), 105–24.

"Some Stages of Logical Thought," *Philosophical Review*, IX (September, 1900), 465–89.

"The Situation as Regards the Course of Study," in National Education Association, Addresses and Proceedings, 1901, pp. 332–48.

"Are the Schools Doing What the People Want Them to Do?" *Educational Review*, XXI (May, 1901), 459–74.

"The Place of Manual Training in the Elementary Course of Study," *Manual Training Magazine*, II (July, 1901), 193–99.

The Child and the Curriculum. Chicago: The University of Chicago Press, 1902. Pp. 40.

The Educational Situation. Chicago: The University of Chicago Press, 1902. Pp. 104.

"The School as Social Center," in National Education Association, Addresses and Proceedings, 1902, pp. 719–20.

"Current Problems of Secondary Education," *School Review*, X (January, 1902), 13–28.

"The Evolutionary Method as Applied to Morality. I. Its Scientific Necessity," *Philosophical Review*, XI (March, 1902), 107–24.

"The Evolutionary Method as Applied to Morality. II. Its Significance for Conduct," *Philosophical Review*, XI (July, 1902), 353–71.

"Interpretation of Savage Mind," *Psychological Review*, IX (May, 1902), 217–30.

Studies in Logical Theory. Chicago: The University of Chicago Press, 1903. Pp. xiii + 388.

"Review of Katherine Elizabeth Dopp, *The Place of Industries in*

Elementary Education," *Elementary School Teacher,* III (June, 1903), 727–28.

"From Absolutism to Experimentalism," in Contemporary American Philosophy. Edited by G. P. Adams and W. P. Montague. Vol. II, London, 1930, pp. 16–20.

A Common Faith. New Haven: Yale University Press, 1934. Pp. 87.

Art as Experience. New York: Minton, Balch and Company, 1935. Pp. vii + 355.

Experience and Education. New York: Macmillan and Company, 1938. Pp. xii + 116.

"Logical Conditions of a Scientific Treatment of Morality," reprinted in John Dewey, Problems of Men, New York: Philosophical Library, 1946, pp. 211–49.

Logic: The Theory of Inquiry. New York: Henry Holt and Company, 1938. Pp. viii + 546.

OTHER SOURCES

Brubacher, John S. A History of the Problems of Education. New York: McGraw-Hill Book Company, Inc., 1947. Pp. xiii + 688.

Butts, R. Freeman. A Cultural History of Education. New York: McGraw-Hill Book Company, Inc., 1947. Pp. ix + 726.

Childs, John. Education and Morals. New York: Appleton-Century-Crofts, Inc., 1950. Pp. xiv + 299.

Curti, Merle. The Growth of American Thought. New York: Harper and Brothers, 1943. Pp. xx + 848.

——— The Social Ideas of American Educators. New York: Charles Scribner's Sons, 1935. Pp. xxii + 613.

DeGarmo, Charles. "Most Pressing Problems Concerning the Elementary Course of Study," in First Yearbook of the National Herbart Society for the Scientific Study of Teaching. Chicago: The University of Chicago Press, 1907, pp. 7–27.

——— "Social Aspects of Moral Education," in Third Yearbook of the National Herbart Society. Chicago: The University of Chicago Press, 1897. Pp. 35–37.

Edwards, Newton, and Herman Richey. The School in the Amer-

ican Social Order. Boston: Houghton Mifflin Company, 1947.
Pp. xiv + 880.

The Forty-First Yearbook of the National Society for the Study of
Education. Chicago: The University of Chicago Press, 1942. Pp.
x + 321.

Galbreath, Louis H. "Discussion," in First Supplement, First Yearbook of the Herbart Society for the Scientific Study of Teaching.
Bloomington, Illinois, 1895. Pp. 141–97.

Harris, W. T. "The Relation of School Discipline to Moral Education," in Third Yearbook of the National Herbart Society.
Chicago: The University of Chicago Press, 1897. Pp. 58–72.

James, William. "Are We Automata?" Mind, IV (1879), 1–12.

McMurry, Frank M. "Concentration," in First Yearbook of the
National Herbart Society for the Scientific Study of Teaching.
Chicago: The University of Chicago Press, 1907, pp. 28–66.

Mayhew, Katherine Camp, and Anna Camp Edwards. The Dewey
School. New York: D. Appleton-Century Company, Inc., 1936.
Pp. xvi + 489.

Mays, Arthur Beverly. "The Concept of Vocational Education in
the Thinking of the General Educator, 1845 to 1945," University of Illinois Bulletin, Vol. 43, No. 65 (July, 1946). Pp. 107.

The Philosophy of John Dewey. Edited by Paul Schilpp. Evanston:
Northwestern University Press, 1939. Pp. 608.

Raup, R. B., G. E. Axtelle, K. D. Benne, and B. O. Smith. The
Improvement of Practical Intelligence. New York: Harper and
Brothers, 1950. Pp. viii + 303.

Rugg, Harold. Foundations for American Education. Yonkers-on-
Hudson, New York: World Book Company, 1947. Pp. xxii +
826.

Schneider, Herbert W. A History of American Philosophy. New
York: Columbia University Press, 1946. Pp. xiv + 646.

Thomas, Milton Halsey, and Herbert Wallace Schneider. A Bibliography of John Dewey. New York: Columbia University Press,
1929. Pp. xxv + 151.

Ulich, Robert. History of Educational Thought. New York:
American Book Co., 1945. Pp. xii + 412.

Van Liew, C. C. "Child Study as Related to Instruction," Trans-
action of the Illinois Society for Child-Study, I, No. 1 (1894).
Pp. 9–21.

—————— "The Educational Theory of the Culture Epochs," in First Yearbook of the National Herbart Society for the Scientific Study of Teaching. Chicago: The University of Chicago Press, 1907, pp. 67–114.

Wahlquist, John T. The Philosophy of American Education. New York: The Ronald Press Company, 1942. Pp. ix + 407.

White, Morton G. The Origin of Dewey's Instrumentalism. New York: Columbia University Press, 1943. Pp. xv + 161.

—————— Social Thought in America. New York: The Viking Press, 1949. Pp. viii + 260.

Wynne, John P. Philosophies of Education from the Standpoint of the Philosophy of Experimentalism. New York: Prentice-Hall, Inc., 1947. Pp. xiv + 427.

INDEX